Collins

Maths

KS2 Maths
SATs Practice Workbook

Age 7 – 11

Key Stage 2

SATs Practice Workbook

Frances Naismith

Contents

Contents

Place Value

Challenge 1

1 Draw **two more** lines to match **4500** to amounts with the same value.

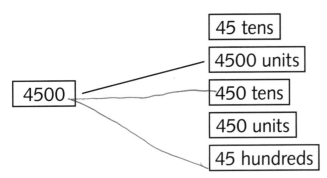

45 tens

4500 units

4500

450 tens

450 units

45 hundreds

2 marks

2 Write these numbers in order from the smallest to the largest.

316   31.6   36.1   3.61   31

Smallest | 3.61 | 31 | 31.6 | 36.1 | 316 | **Largest**

4 marks

3 Circle the numbers with 35 tens.

3527   (2357)   35572   (357)

1 mark

Marks.......... /7

Challenge 2

1 Use > and < to make these statements correct.

a) 19.4 > 18.9   **b)** 67438 < 69436   **c)** 2.357 < 2.537

3 marks

2 Use all of these digit cards to make an odd number whose tens are less than 7.

$3 \times 6 + 8 = 26$

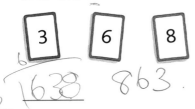

3   6   8

2 1638   863

1 mark

3 Fill in the boxes on the number line.

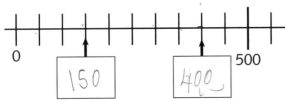

0   150   400   500

2 marks

Marks.......... /6

4

Place Value

Challenge 3

1 What are the next three terms in the sequence?

12 4.5 16.5 4.5 21   _25.5_   _30_   _34.5_

3
3 marks

2 Which is nearer to 300?

279 or 311   _311_

1
1 mark

PS 3 Using each of these five cards once, complete the statements below.

| 3 | 4 | 6 | 8 | 9 |

a) 1 9 6 > 190

b) 3 6 > 3 5

c) 8 6 < 4 4

4
5 marks

4 Fill in the boxes on the number line.

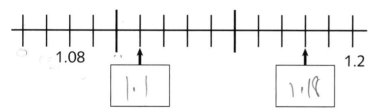

1.08   1.2

1.1   1.18

2 marks

5 Circle the numbers with 32 thousands.

45 329   132 567   56 321.8   432 761.52

1
1 mark

Marks............/12

Negative Numbers

Challenge 1

PS **1** Look at the temperature graph.

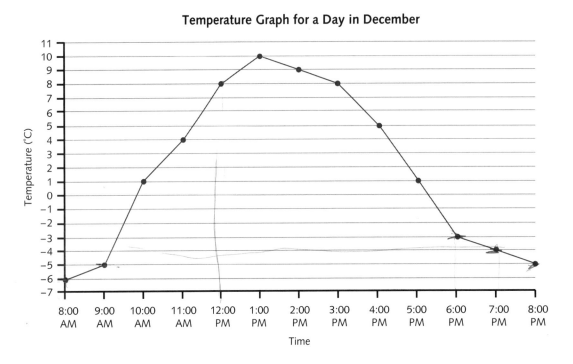

Temperature Graph for a Day in December

a) What temperature is it at 6.00 p.m.?

___−3___ °C

1 mark

b) At 7.00 p.m. the temperature is recorded at −4°C. At 11.00 p.m. it is measured as −12°C.

What is the temperature difference between 7.00 p.m. and 11.00 p.m.?

___−8___ °C ✗ 8

1 mark

c) What is the temperature at A and B?

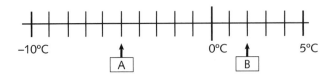

A = ___−5___ °C   B = ___2___ °C

2 marks

Marks..........3..../4

6

Negative Numbers

Challenge 2

 1 **a)** Look at the temperature graph in Challenge 1. Between which two hours did the temperature have the largest increase?

Between ___9___ a.m. and ___10___ a.m.

1 mark

b) In January, the average night temperature is –5°C and the average day temperature is 8°C. What is the temperature difference?

___8___ °C   13

1 mark

2 This sequence is made by **adding the same amount** each time. What are the three missing numbers in the sequence?

–7   17

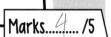
3 marks

Marks.....4..... /5

Challenge 3

 1 **a)** Look at the temperature graph in Challenge 1. What was the temperature difference between 12.00 p.m. and 7.00 p.m.?

___12___ °C

1 mark

b) On how many occasions was the temperature recorded below freezing (0°C)?

___4___ occasions   5

1 mark

c) At midnight the temperature dropped another 6°C from its value recorded at 8.00 p.m. What was the temperature at midnight?

___–11___ °C

1 mark

2 The temperature difference between A and B is 70°C. What is the temperature at A and B?

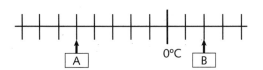
0°C

A = ___–50___ °C

B = ___–20___ °C

2 marks

Marks.....4..... /5

Total marks ....11....... /14   How am I doing?

Rounding

Challenge 1

1   Round 34 612 to the nearest:

   a) 10 _34,600_   **b)** 100 _30,000_   **c)** 1000 _35,000_

   3 marks

2   Circle the number closest to 500.   535   486   (516)

   1 mark

3   Circle the numbers that give 40 when rounded to the nearest 10.

 36   42   45   32   39   35

   2 marks

   Marks.......... /6

Challenge 2

PS ⟩ **1**   Raymond says that if he rounds 247 to the nearest 100 it will round up because 7 is greater than 5.

   Is Raymond correct? _yes_

   1 mark

2   Round 637 261 to the nearest thousand. _640,000_

   1 mark

3   Which is nearer 50? 38 or 61. Give a reason for your answer.

   61 because its only 11 away

   1 mark

   Marks.......... /3

Challenge 3

1   Round 725 345 to the nearest ten thousand. _700,000_

   1 mark

2   What is 5.68 rounded to the nearest whole number? _6_

   1 mark

PS ⟩ **3**   I think of a square number between 20 and 40. I multiply it by 10 and then round it to the nearest 100. My answer is 400.

   What was my number? _40_

   1 mark

   Marks.......... /3

Total marks .... /12   How am I doing?

Roman Numerals

Challenge 1

1   What is 14 in Roman numerals? _____

2   What year do the numerals MM represent? _____

PS 3   What time does the clock show?

_____

1 mark

1 mark

1 mark

Marks.........../3

Challenge 2

1   What do the Roman numerals XXXIX represent? _____

2   Write 48 in Roman numerals. _____

PS 3   Which distance is further,
London or Glasgow?

_____

Glasgow CCXXI miles

London CCLXX miles

1 mark

1 mark

1 mark

Marks.........../3

Challenge 3

1   What year does MCMLXVI represent? _____

PS 2   Fill in the dates on the time line in Roman numerals.

Tudor Times	Great Fire of London	End of World War I	London Olympics	Present Day
	1666	1918	2012	

1 mark

3 marks

Marks.........../4

Total marks ..../10

How am I doing?

Number Facts for Mental Calculations

 PS ⟩ Problem-solving questions

Challenge 1

1 Write the number bonds to 20 for:

    a) 18 _2_   **b)** 4 _16_   **c)** 12 _8_

3 marks

2 **a)** $55 + 9 = 64$ **b)** $43 - 9 = 34$ **c)** $79 + 5 = 84$

3 marks

3 Find the missing numbers.

    a) $34 + \boxed{44} = 88$

    b) $\boxed{74} + 26 = 100$

    c) $\boxed{67} - 17 = 50$

3 marks

Marks.......... /9

Challenge 2

1 Write the number bonds to 100 for:

    a) 68 _32_   **b)** 24 _76_   **c)** 12 _88_

3 marks

2 **a)** $199 + 56 = \underline{245}$

    b) $201 - 85 = \underline{116}$

    c) $302 - 63 = \underline{239}$

3 marks

3 Find the missing numbers.

    a) $34 + \boxed{38} = 72$ **b)** $\boxed{56} + 26 = 82$

    c) $173 - \boxed{67} = 105$ **d)** $111 - \boxed{42} = 79$

    e) $65 + \boxed{37} = 102$ **f)** $\boxed{18} - 58 = 76$

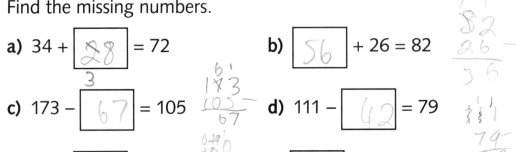

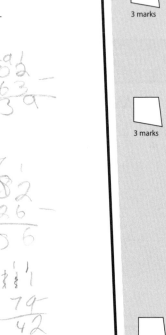

6 marks

Marks......... /12

Number Facts for Mental Calculations

Challenge 3

1 Write the number bonds to 1000 for:

  a) 467 _543_   **b)** 204 _796_   **c)** 365 _645_

$$255+$$
$$39+$$
$$294$$

2 a) 255 + 39 = _294_

  b) 299 – 125 = _174_

  c) 1999 + 63 = _1936_

3 Find the missing numbers.

  a) 1550 + ☐_650_ = 2200

$$2200-$$
$$1550$$
$$0650$$

  b) ☐_1374_ + 126 = 1500

$$1500-$$
$$126$$
$$1374$$

  c) 180 + ☐_3030_ = 3210

$$3210-$$
$$180$$
$$3030$$

  d) 1325 – ☐_1170_ = 155

$$1325-$$
$$155$$
$$1170$$

PS 4 Petra and Mimi each buy a doll. Mimi's doll costs £8.50. Petra gets £2.15 change from £10. How much **more** did Mimi pay than Petra?

  _35_ p

5 Guy has collected 2450 football cards. Reg has 1690. How many cards do the boys have altogether?

  4110 cards

$$2450+$$
$$1690$$
$$4140$$

Marks.........../12

Total marks .... /33   How am I doing?

More Mental Addition and Subtraction

PS ⟩ Problem-solving questions

Challenge 1

1 **a)** 72 – 8 = ___64___   **b)** 127 – 9 = ___118___

2 marks

2 **a)** 210 – 50 = ___160___   **b)** 140 + 30 = ___170___

2 marks

PS ⟩ **3** Shelley has 99p and then finds another 24p in her bag.
How much money does she have now?

£ ___1.23___ or ___123___ p

1 mark

PS ⟩ **4** Kamal spends 38p on sweets. How much change does he get
from £1?

___62___ p

1 mark

PS ⟩ **5** I have 265 football cards. I give 135 to my little brother.

How many do I have left? ___130___

1 mark

Marks.........../7

Challenge 2

1 **a)** 2734 – 1300 = ___40349___   **b)** 1800 + 143 = ___1943___

2 marks

PS ⟩ **2** Greg spends £2.36 on sweets.

How much change does he get from £5?   £ ___2.64___

4 + 9 1
500 –
236
264

1 mark

3 **a)** 1900 – 30 – 180 = ___1850___   **b)** 2400 + 850 = ___3250___

2 marks

PS ⟩ **4** Leanne buys all the stationery supplies on her list below.

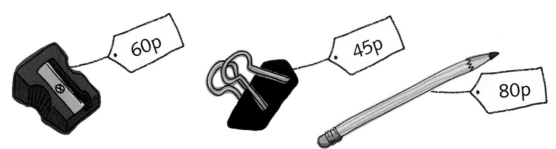

60p   45p   80p

What is her change from £5?   £ ___3.15___ or ___315___ p

2 marks

Marks.........../7

4 + 8 1
500 –
185
315

More Mental Addition and Subtraction

Challenge 3

1 a) 4500 – 950 = _3550_

   b) 8761 – 1000 = _7761_

2 170 + 40 + 150 = _360_

2 marks

1 mark

PS 3 Zamira spends 36p on sweets and 28p on a pencil. How much has she spent?

_56_ p

1 mark

PS 4 Kelly celebrates her 21st birthday in 2019.

In what year was she born? _1997_

1 mark

5 Fill in the missing numbers in the sequence.

132 [ ] [ ] [ ] 68

3 marks

6 How much did Sheila spend on a new coat, bag and gloves?

£8.99   £12.89   £15.99

£ _3687_

1 mark

7 What is the change from £100 for the following amounts?

   a) £36.75 £ _64.25_

   b) £45.54 £ _55.46_

   c) £12.98 £ _8.8.12_

3 marks

Marks.........../12

Total marks ..../26   How am I doing?

Written Addition and Subtraction

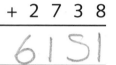
PS Problem-solving questions

Challenge 1

1 a)
```
    3 4 6
  + 1 3 7
  -------
    4 8 3 ✓
```

b)
```
    1 6 8
  + 2 7 5
  -------
    4 4 3 ✓
```

c)
```
    3 4 1 3
  + 2 7 3 8
  ---------
    6 1 5 1 ✓
```

3 marks

2 a)
```
    2 8 4
  - 1 6 2
  -------
    1 2 2 ✓
```

b)
```
    3 5 7
  - 1 6 5
  -------
    1 9 2 ✓
```

c)
```
    1 2.4 5
  -   8.3 1
  ---------
      4.1 4 ✓
```

3 marks

PS 3 The values in the bottom blocks are added together to make the value in the top block. Fill in the blank shapes. The first one has been done for you.

20 / 7 / 13

70 / 18 / 52

130 / 65 / 65

2 marks

Marks.........8.../8

Challenge 2

1 a)
```
    1 9 5
  + 3 4 9
  -------
    5 4 4 ✓
```

b)
```
    4 3 2 7
  + 3 4 8 3   7810
  ---------
    7 4 1 0 ✗
```

c)
```
    5 2.7 5
  + 1 6.8 4
  ---------
    6 9.5 9 ✓
```

3 marks

2 a)
```
    4 3 7
  - 3 6 4
  -------
      7 3 ✓
```

b)
```
    7 1 4 5
  - 2 3 6 6
  ---------
    4 7 7 9 ✓
```

c)
```
    1 6.3 5
  -   9.6 2
  ---------
    6.9 3 ✗
      6. 7 3
```

3 marks

Written Addition and Subtraction

Challenge 2

3 Write two numbers in the boxes to make the statement correct.

70 − [1] = [49] + 20

1 mark

PS 4 Gina saves £34.56. She spends £12.24 on her friend's birthday present. How much money does she have left?

£ _22.32_

1 mark

1 8.1 3 9
− 0 . 5 5
‾‾‾‾‾‾‾
1 . 1 7 4

PS 5 Jill bought three pencils and two rubbers. She spent £2.39. Rubbers cost 55p.

How much did **one** pencil cost? _86_ p

43p.

8 6
2 1 . 7 4

1 mark

Marks.......... /9

Challenge 3

1 a)   3 6 5 7
    + 2 7 6 3
    ‾‾‾‾‾‾‾
    6 4 2 0 ✓

b)   2 7 4 4 5
   +   7 8 4 5
   ‾‾‾‾‾‾‾
   2 5 2 9 0
   3 5 2 9 0 ✗

c)   1 8 9 . 5 6
   +   7 1 . 5 7
   ‾‾‾‾‾‾‾
   2 6 1 0 3 ✗

3 marks

2 a)   9 7 2
   − 5 6 4
   ‾‾‾‾‾
   3 4 8 ✓

b)   6 3 0 5
   − 3 7 1 6
   ‾‾‾‾‾‾
   2 4 8 2 ✗

c)   1 0 . 2 0
   −   3 . 7 9
   ‾‾‾‾‾‾
   6 . 5 1 ✗

3 marks

PS 3 Bailey buys some new football kit:

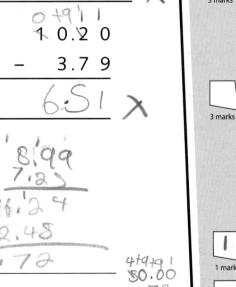

Ball £8.99   Pump £7.25   Shin guards £12.48

8 . 9 9
7 . 2 5
1 2 . 4 8
‾‾‾‾‾‾
2 8 . 7 2

a) How much does he spend altogether? £ _28.72_

1 mark

4 9 9 1
5 0 . 0 0
− 2 8 . 7 2
‾‾‾‾‾‾
2 1 . 2 8

b) What is his change from £50? £ _21.28_

1 mark

Marks.......... /8

Total marks .... /25   How am I doing?   😊   😐   😣

1 What number does XXVIII represent? _____

1 mark

PS **2** Freya bought some shoes, a bag and some earrings for a party.

£23.00   £7.40   £15.50

a) How much did she spend altogether? £ 44.90

1 mark

b) What was her change from £50? £ 5.10

1 mark

3 Order these numbers from smallest to largest.

299   2.90   29.9   29   229

2.90, 29, 29.9, 229, 299

1 mark

4 What value does the digit 3 have in these numbers?

3217   3 thousand

320765   3 hundred thousand

2375   3 hundred

546.3   3 tenths

132.5   3 tens

78.93   3 hundredths

6 marks

PS **5** What are the next three numbers in this sequence?

301   201   101   01   -101   -201

3 marks

6 998 + 34 = 1032

1 mark

7 Each box on the grid should show the sum of the two boxes below it. Fill in the gaps in the grid.

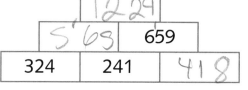

| 1224 |
| 565 | 659 |
| 324 | 241 | 418 |

3 marks

8 What are the number bonds to 100 for the following?

   a) 45 _SS_   **b)** 73 _27_   **c)** 21 _79_

3 marks

9 What is 11 in Roman numerals? _VII_

1 mark

10 Fill in the boxes on the number line.

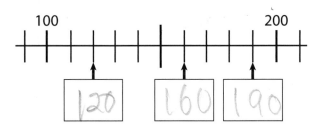

120   160   190

3 marks

11 Double 124 = _248_

1 mark

12 202 − 36 = _66_

```
  202
−  36
─────
   66
```

1 mark

13
```
  1 2 . 3 5
−     8 . 7 2
─────────────
      3 . 8 3
```

1 mark

14 Order these numbers from smallest to largest.

  34 673   43 675   34 763   43 765   34 367

_34367, 34673, 34763, 43675, 43765_

1 mark

15 Round 45 271.5 to the nearest:

  a) ten _45270.0_   **b)** whole number _45272.0_

  c) thousand _50,000_   **d)** hundred _45,300.0_

  e) ten thousand _50,000_

5 marks

16 a)
```
  1 3 5 6
+ 2 6 5 3
─────────
  4 9 0 9
```

    b)
```
  7 6 1 3
− 4 5 2 7
─────────
  3 0 8 7
```

2 marks

Progress Test 1

PS Problem-solving questions

17 1456 + 200 = 1656

1 mark

18 Fill in the gaps on the number line with decimals.

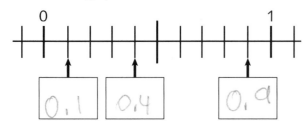

0
1
0.1
0.4
0.9

3 marks

19 How many miles is it to Chester?

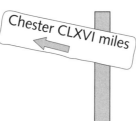

Chester CLXVI miles

____

1 mark

20 Half of 258 = ?

1 mark

21 What is the next number in the sequence?

799 899 999 1099

1 mark

22 What is 12 degrees lower than 3°C? 9 °C

1 mark

23 Circle the estimated answer closest to 32 + 99.

150 100 130 103

1 mark

24 Fill in the gaps on the number line.

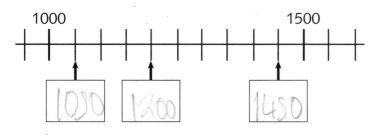

1000
1500
1050
1200
1450

3 marks

25

```
   1 4 . 3 7
 + 2 6 . 3 4
 -----------
   4 0 . 7 1
```

1 mark

26 What are the next three numbers in the sequence?

55   35   15   __−5__   __−25__   __−45__

PS 27 Ben's thermometer reads −5°C and Jake's reads 8°C. What is the temperature difference between the two thermometers?

__12__ °C

28 Each box on the grid holds the difference of the two boxes above it. Fill in the gaps in the grid. One has been done for you.

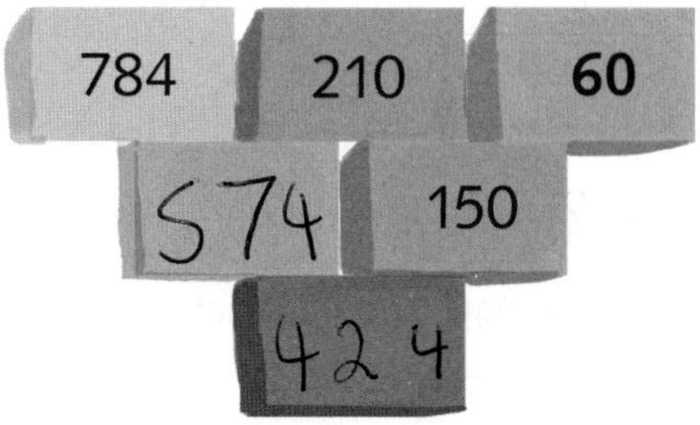

784   210   60

574   150

424

PS 29 Wendy has a new art set. It holds 23 coloured pencils, 28 drawing pencils and 13 watercolour pencils.

a) How many pencils does Wendy have altogether? __64__

b) Wendy lends her friend 11 pencils.
How many pencils does she have left? __53__

PS 30 Jack's new trainers cost £37.55.
Asmir's cost £43.75.

How much more expensive were Asmir's trainers than Jack's?

£ __3.20__

2.59 +
1.25
3.84
87
4 7 1
7 5
3.4 6

PS 31 Jo bought some lunch at the supermarket. Her receipt is shown here.

a) How much did she spend altogether?

£ __5.46__

ALL-U-NEED

Tuna Mayo Wrap £2.59
Energy Drink £1.25
Bacon Crunchies 75p
Choco Bar 87p

Total

b) If she paid with a £20 note, how much change did she get?

£ __14.54__

Marks........./59

All Kinds of Numbers

PS Problem-solving questions

Challenge 1

1   Put the numbers 1 to 20 into the Venn diagram.

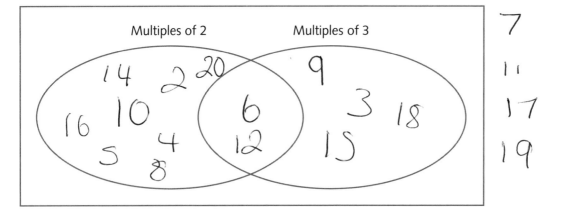

7
11
17
19

4 marks

2   Write two division facts and two multiplication facts using **only** these three numbers.

30 ÷ 6 = 5

30 ÷ 5 = 6   3 ~~⬛⬛⬛~~

2 marks

3   Circle the numbers which are factors of 24.

(3)   5   7   (8)   (6)   (4)   9

2 marks

4   Find a common multiple of 3 and 5. ___15___

1 mark

Marks.......... /9

Challenge 2

1   Circle the factors of 32.

3   (14)   (8)   17   5   12   (4)

1 mark

2   What are the common factors of 24 and 36?

_____

3 marks

3   Find the lowest common multiple of 3, 4 and 6. ___12___

1 mark

Marks.......... /5

All Kinds of Numbers

Challenge 3

1   Here is part of a multiplication grid. Fill in the missing numbers in the blank boxes.

×	6	7	8
5	30	35	40
7	42	49	56
9	54	63	72

4 marks

PS 2   244 is a multiple of 4 **but not** a multiple of 3.

267 is a multiple of 3 **but not** a multiple of 4.

Find a number between 244 and 267 that is a multiple of both **3 and 4**.

_____

1 mark

PS 3   I think of two odd numbers between 30 and 40. They have the common factor 3. What are my numbers?

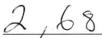 39 and 33

1 mark

4   What is the lowest common multiple of 3, 5 and 7?

_____

1 mark

5   1 and 136 are two factors of 136. Find another two factors of 136.

2, 68

1 mark

Marks.......... /8

Total marks .... /22   How am I doing?

21

Prime, Square and Cube Numbers

PS Problem-solving questions

Challenge 1

1 a) $2^3 =$ ___8___

   b) $4^3 =$ ___48___

   c) $3^2 =$ ___9___

3 marks

2 Circle all the square numbers.

   (32) (16) (24) (36) 9 (45) (25)

2 marks

3 I think of a prime number between 30 and 40.

   Give all the possible answers.

   41, 43, 47, 31, 38

1 mark

4 Use > or < to make the statements correct.

   2^3 [<] 3^2 5^2 [>] 4^2

2 marks

Marks.......... /8

Challenge 2

1 a) $2^2 + 3^2 =$ __13__   b) $4^2 – 2^3 =$ __0__   c) $2^3 + 7^2 =$ __34__

3 marks

2 Circle the prime numbers.

   45 (38) (43) (57) 63 (71) 85

1 mark

3 Use >, < or = to make the statements correct.

   5^2 [<] 4^3

   4^2 [=] 8^2

   6^2 [>] 3^3

3 marks

Marks.......... /7

Prime, Square and Cube Numbers

Challenge 3

1   a) $3^3 + 4^3 - 2^2 =$ ___69___

$3^3 = 9$ $4^3 = 64$ $2^2 = 4$

    b) $5^3 - 7^2 + 2^2 =$ ___72___

$5^3 = \cancel{50125}$ $2^2 = 4$ $\begin{matrix} 16 \times \\ 4 \\ \hline 486 \; 4 \end{matrix}$

$7^2 = \dfrac{49}{7 \; 6}$

 2 marks

PS 2   Complete the boxes.

Prime   Prime
Number   Number

[17] **+** [13] **= 30**

$\begin{matrix} 25 \times \\ 5 \\ \hline 125 \end{matrix}$

 2 marks

3   Put the numbers 1 to 20 into the Venn diagram.

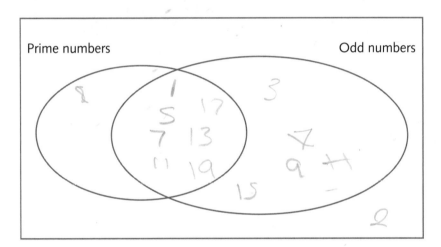

Prime numbers   Odd numbers

8

1
5 17
7 13
11 19

3

7
9 11

15

2

 4 marks

4   Complete the table. The first row has been done for you.

x	x^2	x^3
5	25	125
12	36	432
?	?	729
?	49	?

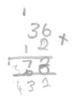 $\begin{matrix} 36 \times \\ 12 \\ \hline 72 \\ 36 \\ \hline 432 \end{matrix}$

3 marks

Marks.......... /11

Multiplying and Dividing

PS Problem-solving questions

Challenge 1

1 **a)** 234 × 10 = _2340_

b) 316 × 100 = _31600_

c) 1567 ÷ 1000 = _1.567_

3 marks

2 Fill in the missing numbers.

a) [10] × 30 = 300

b) 1500 ÷ [100] = 15

c) [10] × 170 = 1700

3 marks

PS **3** Gina buys four chocolate bars that cost 25p each. How much does she pay altogether?

£ _1.00_ or _100_ p

1 mark

Marks.........../7

Challenge 2

1 Fill in the missing numbers.

a) [30.356] × 1000 = 356

b) 245.6 ÷ [10000] = 0.2456

c) [19780] × 100 = 197.8

3 marks

2 **a)** 140 ÷ 70 = _2_

b) 3600 ÷ 6 = _600_

c) 24 × 200 = _480_

3 marks

PS **3** Larry is filling egg boxes with six eggs in each. If he has 84 eggs, how many boxes will he fill?

_14_ boxes

6)84

1 mark

Marks.........../7

Multiplying and Dividing

Challenge 3

1   **a)** 456.2 ÷ 100 = _45.62_

    b) 3.16 × 100 = _316_

    c) 18.37 ÷ 1000 = _0.1837_

3 marks

2   Here are five cards. Use four of them to complete the statements.

| 3.65 | 1000 | 100 | 365 | 10 |

   a) 3650 ÷ [10] = [365]

   b) [3.65] × [1000] = 3650

2 marks

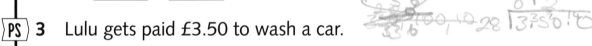

PS **3**   Lulu gets paid £3.50 to wash a car.

      If she earns £28, how many cars has she washed? _____

1 mark

PS **4**   Karl has £38 to spend. If packs of football cards cost £4.25, how many can he buy?

      _____

1 mark

PS **5**   Each week Maya gets £3.25 pocket money and her sister, Jen, gets £2.50. After two weeks the girls put all their money together and buy two equally priced presents for their mum.

      How much does each present cost? £ _5.75_

1 mark

6   2 + 3 × (6 – 2) = _20_

1 mark

7   Bill buys these five books.

      How much does he spend altogether?

£9.25 each

      £ _46.28_

1 mark

Marks........./10

Total marks ..../24   How am I doing? 😊 😐 ☹️

25

Written Multiplication

PS Problem-solving questions

Challenge 1

1 Here is part of a multiplication grid. Fill in the empty boxes.

×	20	
6		24

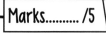
1 mark

2 What is 23 × 35? Use the multiplication grid to help you.

×	20	3
30		
5		

23 × 35 = _____

2 marks

PS 3 A teacher buys 34 new pencils for her class. Each pencil costs 42p.

How much does the teacher spend?

£ _____

1 mark

4
```
    4 3 6
  ×     5
  _____

  _____
```
1 mark

Marks.......... /5

Challenge 2

1 Here is part of a multiplication grid. Fill in the empty boxes.

×	30	
	1200	
5		40

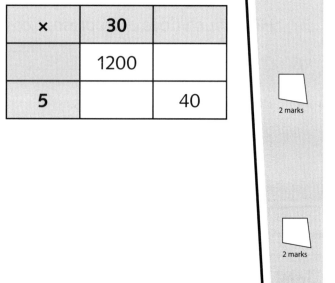
2 marks

2 a)
```
    7 3
  × 2 4
  _____

  _____
```

b)
```
    4 7
  × 3 2
  _____

  _____
```

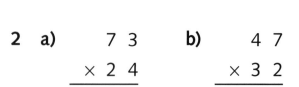
2 marks

Written Multiplication

PS **3** Lily goes to karate club for four weeks.

Is it cheaper to pay monthly or weekly?

_____

Junior Karate Club

Lessons £4.75 per week
Monthly pass £18

1 mark

Marks.......... /5

Challenge 3

1 a)
```
   3 6 4 5
 ×       8
 ─────────

 ─────────
```

b)
```
   3 4 7 5
 ×     2 4
 ─────────

 ─────────

 ─────────
```

2 marks

PS **2** Bike hire costs £3.25 per hour per bike.
Gill pays for herself and four friends to hire
bikes for three hours. What is the total cost?

£ _____

1 mark

PS **3** Mike wants to lay a new path around his garden.
The slabs cost £12.38 each and he needs 28 of them.
How much will his new path cost?

£ _____

1 mark

PS **4** A cat rescue team looks after 23 cats.
Each cat eats a 42p tin of food every day.
How much does it cost to keep the cats
fed for a week?

£ _____

1 mark

Marks.......... /5

Total marks .... /15

How am I doing?

Short and Long Division

PS ⟩ Problem-solving questions

Challenge 1

1 a)

7 | 1 0 5

b)

6 | 2 8 8

2 marks

PS ⟩ 2 Phil, Carrie and Zac share a bag of 126 sweets. How many sweets do the children get each?

_____

1 mark

PS ⟩ 3 Mrs Sprint is organising a football tournament. She has 120 children on her list. If each team has eight children, how many teams will she be able to make?

_____

1 mark

PS ⟩ 4 Jill and Holly put their pocket money together to buy their mum some flowers and chocolates on Mother's Day. How much do the girls pay each if they share the cost equally?

£6.20

£12.50

£ _____

1 mark

Marks.......... /5

Challenge 2

1 a)

9 | 1 6 2

b)

1 7 | 3 7 4

c)

1 1 | 3 2 5

3 marks

28

Short and Long Division

2 Look at the railway season ticket.
How much does each journey cost?

Railway Season Tickets
18 journeys only £396!

£ _____

1 mark

PS **3** Amari is packing crates of water bottles for sports day.
Each crate holds 24 water bottles.

How many crates does she need for 768 bottles?

_____

1 mark

PS **4** Five friends equally split the cost of dinner.
The bill comes to £78.75.

How much do they each pay?

£ _____

1 mark

Marks.......... /6

Challenge 3

1 **a)**

$18\overline{\smash{)}64.8}$

b)

$12\overline{\smash{)}1235}$

2 marks

PS **2** Farmer Biggs needs to buy
some animals for his farm:

Sheep
£5

Cows
£15

If he has £930 to split **equally** between
sheep and cows, how many of each can he buy?

Sheep: _____

Cows: _____

2 marks

Marks.......... /4

Total marks .... /15

How am I doing? 😊 😐 😣

Fractions

Challenge 1

1 What fraction of the shapes is shaded?

a)  $\frac{1}{5}$

b) 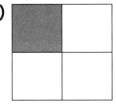 $\frac{1}{4}$

c) 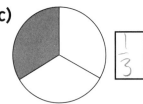 $\frac{1}{3}$

3 marks

2 Simplify these fractions.

a) $\frac{5}{10}$ $\frac{1}{2}$

b) $\frac{8}{24}$ $\frac{1}{4}$

c) $\frac{8}{12}$ $\frac{3}{4}$

3 marks

3 Draw lines to join the equivalent fractions. One has been done for you.

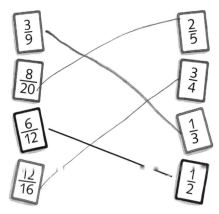

3 marks

4 Shade $\frac{1}{4}$ of these tennis balls.

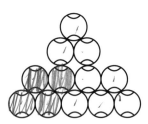

1 mark

Marks.........../10

Challenge 2

PS 1 Order these fractions from the smallest to the largest.

$\frac{3}{4}$ $\frac{1}{8}$ $\frac{1}{2}$ $\frac{1}{4}$

Smallest $\frac{1}{8}$ $\frac{1}{4}$ $\frac{1}{2}$ $\frac{3}{4}$ **Largest**

3 marks

2 Simplify these fractions.

a) $\frac{9}{12}$ $\frac{3}{9}$

b) $\frac{6}{24}$ $\frac{1}{4}$

c) $\frac{6}{45}$

3 marks

3 Shade $\frac{3}{4}$ of these squash balls.

$$\frac{7}{8} \times 2 = \frac{14}{16}$$

$$\frac{3}{4} \times 4 = \frac{12\,16}{16}$$

1 mark

PS **4** Use >, < or = between these pairs of fractions.

a) $\frac{3}{4}$ < $\frac{7}{8}$ b) $\frac{10}{15}$ > $\frac{1}{3}$ c) $\frac{6}{12}$ = $\frac{4}{8}$

$$\frac{4}{8} \times 3 = \frac{12}{24}$$

3 marks

Marks......... /10

Challenge 3

PS **1** Farmer Green has 24 cows.

$\frac{3}{8}$ are black, $\frac{1}{6}$ are brown, $\frac{3}{12}$ are spotted and the rest are white.

Shade the cows to show the number of each colour.

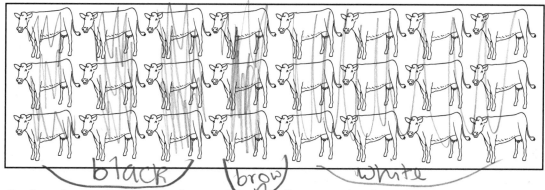

black   brow   white

3 marks

PS **2** Order these fractions from the smallest to the largest.

$$\frac{6}{12} \qquad \frac{3}{4} \qquad \frac{3}{8} \qquad \frac{1}{4} \qquad \frac{5}{8}$$

Smallest $\boxed{\frac{1}{4}}$ $\boxed{\frac{3}{8}}$ $\boxed{\frac{5}{8}}$ $\boxed{\frac{6}{12}}$ $\boxed{\frac{3}{4}}$ **Largest**

4 marks

PS **3** Use >, < or = between these pairs of fractions.

a) $\frac{25}{30}$ > $\frac{10}{25}$ b) $\frac{12}{18}$ > $\frac{30}{45}$ c) $\frac{16}{28}$ < $\frac{9}{15}$

3 marks

Marks......... /10

Total marks .... /30   How am I doing?

Adding, Subtracting, Multiplying and Dividing Fractions

Challenge 1

1 a) $\frac{2}{7} + \frac{3}{7}$ = $\boxed{\frac{5}{7}}$ b) $\frac{3}{12} + \frac{4}{12}$ = $\boxed{\frac{7}{12}}$ c) $\frac{3}{5} + \frac{4}{5}$ = $\boxed{\frac{7}{5}}$

 3 marks

2 a) $\frac{6}{15} - \frac{3}{15}$ = $\boxed{\frac{3}{15}}$ b) $\frac{9}{12} - \frac{4}{12}$ = $\boxed{\frac{3}{12}}$ c) $\frac{12}{10} - \frac{1}{10}$ = $\boxed{\frac{11}{10}}$

 3 marks

3 a) $\frac{1}{3} \times \frac{1}{4}$ = $\boxed{\frac{1}{12}}$ b) $\frac{1}{5} \times \frac{1}{3}$ = $\boxed{\frac{1}{15}}$ c) $\frac{1}{7} \times \frac{1}{2}$ = $\boxed{\frac{1}{14}}$

 3 marks

4 a) $\frac{1}{4} \div 2$ = $\boxed{\frac{1}{8}}$ b) $\frac{1}{2} \div 2$ = $\boxed{\frac{1}{4}}$ c) $\frac{1}{5} \div 2$ = $\boxed{\frac{1}{10}}$

 3 marks

Marks.........../12

Challenge 2

1 a) $\frac{1}{5} + \frac{1}{10}$ = $\boxed{\frac{2}{20}}$ b) $\frac{1}{4} + \frac{1}{2}$ = $\boxed{\frac{3}{4}}$ c) $\frac{1}{4} + \frac{1}{8}$ = $\boxed{\frac{3}{8}}$

 3 marks

2 a) $\frac{6}{10} - \frac{1}{5}$ = $\boxed{\frac{4}{10}}$ b) $\frac{9}{12} - \frac{1}{6}$ = $\boxed{\frac{7}{12}}$ c) $\frac{3}{4} - \frac{1}{2}$ = $\boxed{\frac{1}{4}}$

 3 marks

3 a) $\frac{1}{3} \times \frac{1}{9}$ = $\boxed{\frac{1}{27}}$ b) $\frac{1}{5} \times \frac{1}{7}$ = $\boxed{\frac{1}{35}}$ c) $\frac{1}{9} \times \frac{1}{12}$ = $\boxed{\frac{1}{108}}$

 3 marks

4 a) $\frac{1}{8} \div 2$ = $\boxed{\frac{1}{16}}$ b) $\frac{1}{10} \div 2$ = $\boxed{\frac{1}{20}}$ c) $\frac{1}{15} \div 2$ = $\boxed{\frac{1}{30}}$

 3 marks

Marks.........../12

Challenge 3

1 a) $\frac{2}{6} + \frac{1}{4}$ = $\boxed{\frac{7}{12}}$ b) $\frac{3}{4} + \frac{1}{3}$ = $\boxed{\frac{6}{12}}$ c) $\frac{3}{7} + \frac{1}{3}$ = $\boxed{}$

 3 marks

2 a) $\frac{6}{15} - \frac{1}{5}$ = $\boxed{\frac{3}{15}}$ b) $\frac{9}{12} - \frac{1}{6}$ = $\boxed{\frac{7}{12}}$ c) $\frac{8}{10} - \frac{1}{4}$ = $\boxed{}$

 3 marks

3 a) $\frac{1}{12} \times \frac{1}{7}$ = $\boxed{\frac{1}{84}}$ b) $\frac{1}{8} \times \frac{1}{15}$ = $\boxed{\frac{1}{480}}$ c) $\frac{1}{13} \times \frac{1}{5}$ = $\boxed{}$

 3 marks

4 a) $\frac{1}{2} \div 4$ = $\boxed{\frac{1}{8}}$ b) $\frac{1}{12} \div 3$ = $\boxed{\frac{1}{4}}$ c) $\frac{1}{25} \div 2$ = $\boxed{}$

 3 marks

Marks.........../12

Total marks ..../36   How am I doing?

Decimal Fractions

Challenge 1

1 Write these fractions as decimals.

a) $\frac{1}{4}$ _0.25_   b) $\frac{3}{4}$ _0.75_   c) $\frac{1}{2}$ _0.5_

3 marks

2 Fill in the boxes on the number line.

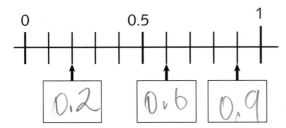

0   0.5   1

_0.2_   _0.6_   _0.9_

3 marks

3 Round these decimals to the nearest whole number.

a) 45.6 _46_   b) 243.2 _243_   c) 1.62 _2_

3 marks

Marks........... /9

Challenge 2

1 Write these fractions as decimals.

a) $\frac{1}{8}$ _0.125_   b) $1\frac{3}{4}$ _1.75_   c) $\frac{1}{1000}$ _0.001_

3 marks

2 Fill in the missing numbers.

_0.0345_ × 100 = 3.45   67.34 ÷ _10_ = 6.734

2 marks

Marks........... /5

Challenge 3

1 Order these decimals from the smallest to the largest.

3.41   3.4   304.1   34.1   3.04

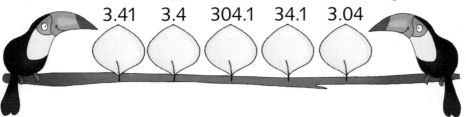

1 mark

2 Round these to one decimal place.

a) 45.64 _45.6_   b) 243.27 _243.3_   c) 1.95 _2.0_

3 marks

Marks........... /4

Total marks .... /18   How am I doing?

Improper Fractions and Mixed Numbers

 PS Problem-solving questions

Challenge 1

1 $1\frac{3}{4}$ is a mixed number.

What mixed numbers do these represent?

a)  $1\frac{1}{2}$ b)  $2\frac{1}{4}$ c)  $2\frac{3}{4}$

3 marks

2 Put a tick (✓) beside the fractions greater than 1 and a cross (✗) beside the fractions less than 1.

$\frac{4}{5}$ ✗ $\frac{7}{6}$ ✓ $1\frac{1}{2}$ ✓ $\frac{2}{3}$ ✗ $\frac{5}{4}$ ✓

5 marks

Marks.......... /8

Challenge 2

1 What improper fractions do these represent?

a) ☐   b) $\frac{2}{1}$ c)  $\frac{3}{1}$

3 marks

2 Convert these improper fractions to mixed numbers.

a) $\frac{11}{6}$ $1\frac{5}{6}$ b) $\frac{14}{3}$ $4\frac{2}{3}$ c) $\frac{15}{4}$ _____

3 marks

Marks.......... /6

Challenge 3

1 Give your answers as mixed numbers.

a) $\frac{9}{5} + \frac{2}{5} =$ $1\frac{2}{5}$ b) $\frac{7}{8} + \frac{7}{8} =$ $1\frac{6}{8}$ c) $\frac{4}{5} + \frac{6}{5} + \frac{3}{5} =$ $2\frac{3}{5}$

3 marks

2 Use >, < or = to make these statements correct.

a) $\frac{15}{6}$ < $\frac{5}{2}$ b) $1\frac{4}{5}$ < $\frac{11}{5}$

2 marks

Marks.......... /5

Total marks .... /19   How am I doing?

34

Percentages

Challenge 1

1 What are the percentages represented by these fractions?

a) $\frac{1}{4}$ _0.25%_   b) $\frac{3}{4}$ _0.75%_   c) $\frac{1}{2}$ _0.50%_.

3 marks

2 Find:

a) 25% of 36 _14_   b) 50% of 128 _64_   c) 75% of 60 _45_

3 marks

$2.5\overline{)36\cdot0}$ _01:4_   0 25, 50, 75, 100

Marks.......... /6

Challenge 2

1 Find:

a) 10% of 125 _12.5_   b) 30% of 120 _25_   c) 80% of 60 _45_

3 marks

PS 2 Last year my rail card cost £32. This year the price has **increased** by 20%. How much will my rail card cost this year?

£ _____

1 mark

Marks.......... /4

Challenge 3

PS 1 Peter got $\frac{15}{20}$ for his Maths test and $\frac{18}{25}$ for his Geography test.

Which subject did he do better in? _Geography_

1 mark

2 Use >, < or = to make these statements correct.

a) $\frac{24}{40}$ ☐ $\frac{21}{30}$ b) $\frac{8}{20}$ ☐ $\frac{24}{60}$ c) $\frac{4}{25}$ ☐ $\frac{7}{50}$

3 marks

PS 3 Next year house prices are set to rise by 15%. If my house cost £135 000 this year, how much will it be worth next year?

£ _____

1 mark

Marks.......... /5

Total marks .... /15

How am I doing?

35

1 Circle the prime numbers.

12   (17)   (19)   (26)   (43)   (57)   85   (97)

2 marks

2 $\frac{1}{3} \times \frac{1}{2} =$ ☐

1 mark

3 Put all the numbers from 1 to 20 into the diagram.

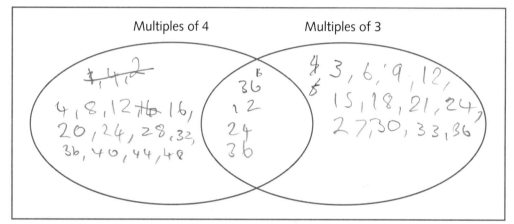

Multiples of 4   Multiples of 3

~~1,4,2~~

4, 8, 12 ~~16,~~ 16,
20, 24, 28, 32,
36, 40, 44, 48

36
12
24
36

~~4~~ 3, 6, 9, 12,
~~8~~ 15, 18, 21, 24,
27, 30, 33, 36,

4 marks

4 $\frac{12}{16} - \frac{3}{8} = \boxed{\frac{6}{16}}$

1 mark

5 a)

```
  8 6 3 . 4
+   8 9 . 8
-----------
    9 4 3 2
```

b)

```
  1 2 1 . 3
-   3 7 . 8
-----------
    4 3 . 5
```

2 marks

6 Complete the multiplication grid.

×	7	9	12
8	54	72	96
12	84	108	108
5	35	45	60

4 marks

7 Convert $1\frac{5}{8}$ to an improper fraction. ☐

1 mark

8 Find 70% of 120. _65_

9 $7^2 =$ _42_

10 Write < or > between these numbers: 98 765 [<] 987 650

11 Circle the square numbers.

 16 32 25 44 64

12 $\frac{1}{4} \div 4 =$ [$\frac{1}{16}$]

13 Convert $\frac{18}{12}$ to a mixed number. _$1\frac{4}{12}$_

14 $4^2 + 3^3 =$ _25_

15 Work this out, giving your remainder as a fraction.

$7\overline{)1\,2\,9}$ → $0\,1\,7$

16 $\frac{3}{12} + \frac{1}{4} + \frac{2}{3} =$ [$\frac{17}{12}$]

$6+8$

17 Convert $\frac{9}{20}$ to a percentage. _45%_

18 List all the factors of 24. _1, 2, 3, 6, 8, 12, 24_

19 Complete this sequence:

15 , 11 , 7 , 3 _0-1_ _-5_ _-9_

20   2 4
    × 4 6
    ————
    ————

21 Round 956 to the nearest hundred. _____

 1 mark
 1 mark
 1 mark
 1 mark
 1 mark
 1 mark
 1 mark

 1 mark
 1 mark

4 marks

3 marks

 1 mark

1 mark

PS **22** A sports shop is having a sale. Trainers are **reduced** by 25%.
If the original price was £80, what is the sale price?

£ _____

1 mark

23 What year do the numerals MMXVI represent? _2106_
2 10V

1 mark

PS **24** Look at the items at the garden centre.

£4.25 per packet   £6.18   £8.95 each

a) How many plants can Julie buy for £30? _____

1 mark

b) If Jai buys seven forks, how much has he spent? £ _____

1 mark

c) Amelia spends exactly £46.75 on seeds.

How many packets of seeds did she buy? _____

1 mark

d) If plants are on a special offer of 'Buy two get one free',
how much does each of the three plants actually cost?

£ _____

1 mark

25 £6700 + £ | 2300 | = £9000

1 mark

26 Circle the cube numbers.

5   8   12   25   27   36

2 marks

27 Write $1\frac{1}{4}$ as a decimal. _1.25_

1 mark

28 Work this out, giving your
answer with a remainder.   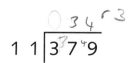

$11\overline{)3779}$ 0 3 4 r 3

1 mark

29 1900 – 750 – 340 = _710_

1 mark

30 Which is greater, $\frac{4}{5}$ or $\frac{2}{3}$? $\frac{2}{3}$

1 mark

PS **31** Draw lines to join the equivalent fractions. One has been done for you.

$\frac{16}{20}$ $1\frac{3}{7}$ $\frac{1}{4}$ $\frac{18}{30}$ $\frac{6}{21}$

$\frac{20}{14}$ $\frac{4}{5}$ $\frac{2}{7}$ $\frac{3}{5}$ $\frac{8}{32}$

4 marks

32 Round 1549 894 to the nearest 100 000. 150,000

1 mark

33 Ali has a box of chocolates. He gives seven of his friends five chocolates each. He has six chocolates left.

How many chocolates were in the box? 42

1 mark

34 $2^2 + 4^3 - 3^2 =$ 75

66   9

1 mark

35 What are the common multiples of 3 and 4 (between 1 and 30)?

1, 12, 6, 8, 16

2 marks

PS **36** 18 out of a class of 30 children are girls. What percentage are girls?

~~72~~ 55%

1 mark

PS **37** Look at this sign advertising boat hire.

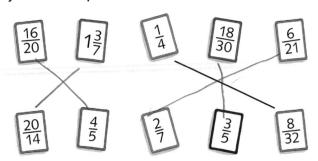

Boat Hire
£7.75 per hour
or 4 hours
for £30

$\begin{array}{r} \overset{3}{7}.\overset{2}{7}5 \times \\ 4 \\ \hline 3\cancel{0}\ 0\ 0 \end{array}$

a) Carl wants to hire a boat for four hours.

Is it cheaper to pay by the hour or take the four-hour deal?

The four hour deal.

1 mark

b) Geeta hired a boat for six hours and paid by the hour.

How much did she pay? £ 46.50

$\begin{array}{r} \overset{4}{7}.7\overset{3}{5} \times \\ 6 \\ \hline 46.50 \end{array}$

1 mark

c) Johnny has £40 to spend. How many hours can he hire a boat for at the hourly rate?

18

$\begin{array}{r} 1.8 \\ 4\overline{)7.\overset{3}{7}\overset{5}{5}} \end{array}$

1 mark

Marks........ /60

Units of Measurement

Challenge 1

1 Write the units under the correct headings. One has been done for you.

centimetres   litres   minutes   metres   grams
kilometres   seconds   millilitres   hours   kilograms

Length	Volume/ Capacity	Weight	Time
millimetres			

4 marks

2 Convert these measures.

a) 10 cm = _____ mm   b) 3 kg = _____ g

c) 500 cm = _____ m   d) 120 seconds = _____ mins

4 marks

PS 3 I pour 250 ml squash into my jug. How much more do I need to pour in to fill it up to the 1 litre mark?

_____ ml

1 mark

Marks.......... /9

Challenge 2

1 Complete the blank squares in the grid.

mm	cm	m	km
		255	
36			
			4.78
	123		

6 marks

2 Put a circle around the correct answer.

A mug of tea holds approximately   25 ml   2.5 l   250 ml   2.5 ml

1 mark

Pages 4–5
Challenge 1
1

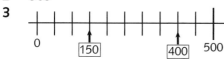

          45 tens
          4500 units
4500 — 450 tens
          450 units
          45 hundreds

2   smallest 3.61 | 31 | 31.6 | 36.1 | 316 largest
3   3527 (2357) 35572 (357)

Challenge 2
1 **a)** 19.4 > 18.9   **b)** 67 438 < 69 436
   c) 2.357 < 2.537
2 863
3

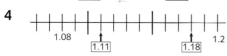

0 ... 150 ... 400 500

Challenge 3
1 25.5   30   34.5
2 311
3 **a)** 1 | 9 | 6 > 190
   b) 3 | 6   > 3 | 5
   c) 4 | 6 < 4 | 8
4

1.08 ... 1.11 ... 1.18 ... 1.2

5 45 329 (132 567) 56 321.8 (432 761.52)

Pages 6–7
Challenge 1
1 **a)** −3°C
   b) 8°C
   c) A = −5°C   B = 2°C

Challenge 2
1 **a)** 9 a.m. and 10 a.m.
   b) 13°C
2 −1, 5, 11

Challenge 3
1 **a)** 12°C
   b) 5 occasions
   c) −11°C
2 A = −50°C   B = 20°C

Page 8
Challenge 1
1 **a)** 34 610   **b)** 34 600   **c)** 35 000
2 535 (486) 516
3 (36) (42) 45 32 (39) (35)

Challenge 2
1 No (He is looking at the units instead of the tens. 247 will round down because the tens digit is a 4.)
2 637 000
3 61 (it's 11 away from 50; 38 is 12 away from 50)

Challenge 3
1 730 000
2 6
3 36

Page 9
Challenge 1
1 XIV
2 2000
3 4:35

Challenge 2
1 39
2 XLVIII
3 London – 270 miles (Glasgow 221 miles)

Challenge 3
1 1966
2

1666	1918	2012
MDCLXVI	MCMXVIII	MMXII

Pages 10–11
Challenge 1
1 **a)** 2   **b)** 16   **c)** 8
2 **a)** 64   **b)** 34   **c)** 84
3 **a)** 54   **b)** 74   **c)** 67

Challenge 2
1 **a)** 32   **b)** 76   **c)** 88
2 **a)** 255   **b)** 116   **c)** 239
3 **a)** 38   **b)** 56   **c)** 68
   d) 32   **e)** 37   **f)** 134

Challenge 3
1 **a)** 533 **b)** 796   **c)** 635
2 **a)** 294 **b)** 174   **c)** 2062
3 **a)** 650 **b)** 1374 **c)** 3030   **d)** 1170
4 65p
5 4140

Pages 12–13
Challenge 1
1 **a)** 64   **b)** 118
2 **a)** 160   **b)** 170
3 £1.23 or 123p
4 62p
5 130

Answers

Challenge 2
1. a) 1434　　b) 1943
2. £2.64
3. a) 1690　　b) 3250
4. £3.15 or 315p

Challenge 3
1. a) 3550　　b) 7761
2. 360
3. 64p
4. 1998
5. 116, 100, 84
6. £37.87
7. a) £63.25　　b) £54.46　　c) £87.02

Pages 14–15
Challenge 1
1. a) 483　　b) 443　　c) 6151
2. a) 122　　b) 192　　c) 4.14
3.
70		130	
18	52	65	65

Challenge 2
1. a) 544　　b) 7810　　c) 69.59
2. a) 73　　b) 4779　　c) 6.73
3. Any two numbers which total 50, e.g. 1, 49; 2, 48…
4. £22.32
5. 43p

Challenge 3
1. a) 6420　　b) 35290　　c) 261.13
2. a) 348　　b) 2589　　c) 6.41
3. a) £28.72　　b) £21.28

Pages 16–19
Progress Test 1
1. 28
2. a) £45.90　　b) £4.10
3. 2.90　29　29.9　229　299
4. thousands
   hundred thousands
   hundreds
   tenths
   tens
   hundredths
5. 1, −99, −199
6. 1032
7.
	1224	
565	659	
324	241	418
8. a) 55　　b) 27　　c) 79
9. XI

10.

11. 248
12. 166
13. 3.63
14. 34367　34673　34763　43675　43765
15. a) 45270
    b) 45272
    c) 45000
    d) 45300
    e) 50000
16. a) 4009　　b) 3086
17. 1656
18.

19. 166
20. 129
21. 1099
22. −9°C
23. 150　100　(130)　103
24.

25. 40.71
26. −5, −25, −45
27. 13°C
28.
784	210	60
574	150	
424		
29. a) 64　　b) 53
30. £6.20
31. a) £5.46　　b) £14.54

Pages 20–21
Challenge 1
1.

2. 6 × 5 = 30; 5 × 6 = 30; 30 ÷ 5 = 6; 30 ÷ 6 = 5
3. (3) 5 7 (8) (6) (4) 9
4. 15, 30, 45, 60 etc.

Challenge 2
1 3 14 ⑧ 17 5 12 ④
2 1, 2, 3, 4, 6, 12
3 12

Challenge 3
1

×	6	7	8
5	30	35	40
7	42	49	56
9	54	63	72

2 252 or 264
3 33 and 39
4 105
5 2, 68; 4, 34; or 8, 17

Pages 22–23
Challenge 1
1 a) 8 b) 64 c) 9
2 32 ⑯ 24 ㊱ ⑨ 45 ㉕
3 31, 37
4 $2^3 < 3^2$
  $5^2 > 4^2$

Challenge 2
1 a) 13 b) 8 c) 57
2 45 38 ㊸ 57 63 ㉛ 85
3 $5^2 < 4^3$
  $4^2 < 8^2$
  $6^2 > 3^3$

Challenge 3
1 a) 87 b) 80
2 7 + 23 or 11 + 19 or 13 + 17

3

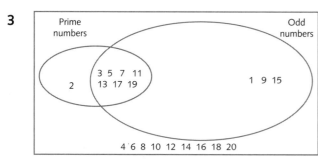

Prime numbers: 2 | 3 5 7 11 13 17 19 | Odd numbers: 1 9 15
4 6 8 10 12 14 16 18 20

4

x	x^2	x^3
5	25	125
6	36	216
9	81	729
7	49	343

Pages 24–25
Challenge 1
1 a) 2340 b) 31 600 c) 1.567
2 a) 10 × 30 = 300
  b) 1500 ÷ 100 = 15
  c) 10 × 170 = 1700
3 £1.00 or 100p

Challenge 2
1 a) 0.356 × 1000 = 356
  b) 245.6 ÷ 1000 = 0.2456
  c) 1.978 × 100 = 197.8
2 a) 2 b) 600 c) 4800
3 14 boxes

Challenge 3
1 a) 4.562 b) 316.0 c) 0.01837
2 a) 3650 ÷ 1000 = 3.65 or
    3650 ÷ 365 = 10 or
    3650 ÷ 10 = 365 or
    3650 ÷ 3.65 = 1000
  b) 365 × 10 = 3650 or
     3.65 × 1000 = 3650 or
     10 × 365 = 3650 or
     1000 × 3.65 = 3650
3 8
4 8
5 £5.75 **6** 14 **7** £46.25

Pages 26–27
Challenge 1
1

×	20	4
6	120	24

2

×	20	3
30	600	90
5	100	15

Total = 805

3 £14.28 **4** 2180

Challenge 2
1

×	30	8
40	1200	320
5	150	40

2 a) 1752 b) 1504
3 4 weeks = £19. Cheaper to pay monthly by £1

Answers

Challenge 3
1. a) 29 160
   b) 83 400
2. £48.75
3. £346.64
4. £67.62

Pages 28–29
Challenge 1
1. a) 15   b) 48
2. 42
3. 15
4. £9.35

Challenge 2
1. a) 18   b) 22   c) 29 r6 or $29\frac{6}{11}$
2. £22
3. 32
4. £15.75

Challenge 3
1. a) 3.6   b) 102 r11 or $102\frac{11}{12}$
2. 93 sheep and 31 cows

Pages 30–31
Challenge 1
1. a) $\frac{1}{5}$ b) $\frac{1}{4}$ c) $\frac{1}{3}$
2. a) $\frac{1}{2}$ b) $\frac{1}{3}$ c) $\frac{2}{3}$
3.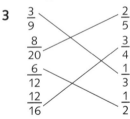
   $\frac{3}{9}$, $\frac{8}{20}$, $\frac{6}{12}$, $\frac{12}{16}$; $\frac{2}{5}$, $\frac{3}{4}$, $\frac{1}{3}$, $\frac{1}{2}$
4. Three balls shaded

Challenge 2
1. $\boxed{\frac{1}{8}}$ $\boxed{\frac{1}{4}}$ $\boxed{\frac{1}{2}}$ $\boxed{\frac{3}{4}}$
2. a) $\frac{3}{4}$ b) $\frac{1}{4}$ c) $\frac{2}{15}$
3. Nine balls shaded
4. a) $\frac{3}{4} < \frac{7}{8}$
   b) $\frac{10}{15} > \frac{1}{3}$
   c) $\frac{6}{12} = \frac{4}{8}$

Challenge 3
1. Shaded: 9 black, 4 brown, 6 spotted and 5 white
2. $\boxed{\frac{1}{4}}$ $\boxed{\frac{3}{8}}$ $\boxed{\frac{6}{12}}$ $\boxed{\frac{5}{8}}$ $\boxed{\frac{3}{4}}$
3. a) $\frac{25}{30} > \frac{10}{25}$
   b) $\frac{12}{18} = \frac{30}{45}$
   c) $\frac{16}{28} < \frac{9}{15}$

Page 32
Challenge 1
1. a) $\frac{5}{7}$ b) $\frac{7}{12}$ c) $\frac{7}{5}$
2. a) $\frac{3}{15}$ b) $\frac{5}{12}$ c) $\frac{11}{10}$
3. a) $\frac{1}{12}$ b) $\frac{1}{15}$ c) $\frac{1}{14}$
4. a) $\frac{1}{8}$ b) $\frac{1}{4}$ c) $\frac{1}{10}$

Challenge 2
1. a) $\frac{3}{10}$ b) $\frac{3}{4}$ c) $\frac{3}{8}$
2. a) $\frac{4}{10}$ or $\frac{2}{5}$ b) $\frac{7}{12}$ c) $\frac{1}{4}$
3. a) $\frac{1}{27}$ b) $\frac{1}{35}$ c) $\frac{1}{108}$
4. a) $\frac{1}{16}$ b) $\frac{1}{20}$ c) $\frac{1}{30}$

Challenge 3
1. a) $\frac{7}{12}$ b) $\frac{13}{12}$ c) $\frac{16}{21}$
2. a) $\frac{3}{15}$ or $\frac{1}{5}$ b) $\frac{7}{12}$ c) $\frac{11}{20}$
3. a) $\frac{1}{84}$ b) $\frac{1}{120}$ c) $\frac{1}{65}$
4. a) $\frac{1}{8}$ b) $\frac{1}{36}$ c) $\frac{1}{50}$

Page 33
Challenge 1
1. a) 0.25   b) 0.75   c) 0.5
2.
3. a) 46   b) 243   c) 2

Challenge 2
1. a) 0.125   b) 1.75   c) 0.001
2. $\boxed{0.0345} \times 100 = 3.45$
   $67.34 \div \boxed{10} = 6.734$

Challenge 3
1 3.04   3.4   3.41   34.1   304.1
2 **a)** 45.6   **b)** 243.3   **c)** 2.0

Page 34
Challenge 1
1 **a)** $1\frac{1}{2}$ **b)** $2\frac{1}{4}$ **c)** $2\frac{3}{4}$
2 $\frac{4}{5} \times \frac{7}{6}$ ✓ $1\frac{1}{2}$ ✓ $\frac{2}{3} \times \frac{5}{4}$ ✓

Challenge 2
1 **a)** $\frac{15}{4}$ **b)** $\frac{15}{6}$ **c)** $\frac{10}{3}$
2 **a)** $1\frac{5}{6}$ **b)** $4\frac{2}{3}$ **c)** $3\frac{3}{4}$

Challenge 3
1 **a)** $2\frac{1}{5}$ **b)** $1\frac{6}{8}$ or $1\frac{3}{4}$ **c)** $2\frac{3}{5}$
2 **a)** $\frac{15}{6} = \frac{5}{2}$
    b) $1\frac{4}{5} < \frac{11}{5}$

Page 35
Challenge 1
1 **a)** 25%   **b)** 75%   **c)** 50%
2 **a)** 9   **b)** 64   **c)** 45

Challenge 2
1 **a)** 12.5   **b)** 36   **c)** 48
2 £38.40

Challenge 3
1 Maths (75%, Geography, 72%)
2 **a)** $\frac{24}{40} < \frac{21}{30}$
    b) $\frac{8}{20} = \frac{24}{60}$
    c) $\frac{4}{25} > \frac{7}{50}$
3 £155 250

Pages 36–39

Progress Test 2
1 12 ⑰ ⑲ 26 ㊸ 57 85 ㊙
2 $\frac{1}{6}$

3
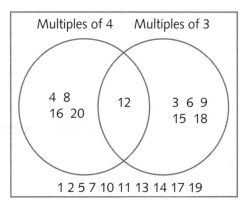

4 $\frac{6}{16}$ or $\frac{3}{8}$
5 **a)** 953.2   **b)** 83.5

6

×	7	9	12
8	56	72	96
9	63	81	108
5	35	45	60

7 $\frac{13}{8}$
8 84
9 49
10 98 765 < 987 650
11 ⑯ 32 ㉕ 44 ㉚
12 $\frac{1}{16}$
13 $1\frac{6}{12}$ or $1\frac{1}{2}$
14 43
15 $18\frac{3}{7}$
16 $\frac{14}{12}$ or $\frac{7}{6}$ or $1\frac{1}{6}$
17 45%
18 1, 24, 2, 12, 3, 8, 4, 6
19 15, 11, 7, 3, −1, −5, −9
20 1104
21 1000
22 £60
23 2016
24 **a)** 4
    b) £62.65
    c) 11
    d) £4.12
25 £2300
26 5 ⑧ 12 25 ㉗ 36
27 1.25
28 34 r5

Answers

29 810

30 $\frac{4}{5}$

31

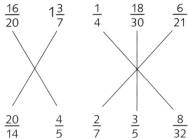

$\frac{16}{20}$ $1\frac{3}{7}$ $\frac{1}{4}$ $\frac{18}{30}$ $\frac{6}{21}$

$\frac{20}{14}$ $\frac{4}{5}$ $\frac{2}{7}$ $\frac{3}{5}$ $\frac{8}{32}$

32 1 500 000

33 41

34 59

35 12, 24

36 60%

37 a) Four-hour deal (4hrs = £31)
    b) £46.50
    c) 5

Pages 40–41
Challenge 1

1

Length	Volume / Capacity	Weight	Time
millimetres centimetres metres kilometres	litres millilitres	grams kilograms	minutes seconds hours

2 a) 100 mm   b) 3000 g   c) 5 m   d) 2 mins

3 750 ml

Challenge 2

1

mm	cm	m	km
	25 500	255	0.255
36	3.6		
		4780	4.78
1230	123	1.23	

2 25 ml   2.5 l   250 ml   2.5 ml

3 633 m

4 300 g

Challenge 3

1 20 cm

2 2 m   B
   0.5 m   A
   $4\frac{1}{2}$ m   D
   300 cm   C

---

3 b) 5 miles   8 m   80 km   8 km
   c) 4 inches   1 cm   100 cm   10 cm

Pages 42–43
Challenge 1

1 P = 6 cm
2 P = 24 m
3 A = 100 cm²

Challenge 2

1 P = 34 cm
2 A = 300 m²
3 P = 46 m

Challenge 3

1 a) 28 m
   b) 42 m²
2 7 cm and 5 cm or 1 cm and 35 cm

Pages 44–45
Challenge 1

1 31.5 cm²
2 5p   51p   £5   501p   551p
3 V = 27 cm³

Challenge 2

1 40 cm²
2 160 cm³
3 20p, 5p, 5p, 5p, 2p

Challenge 3

1 3 cm
2 55 cm²
3 Any amount from 35p to 44p
4 112 cm³

Pages 46–47
Challenge 1

1 a) A clock face shows **12** hours.
      There are **24** hours in one day.
   b) Each hour is **60** minutes long. Two minutes
      equals **120** seconds.
   c) There are usually **365** days in a year.
      June has **30** days.
2 8.20 a.m.
3 6.20 p.m.

Challenge 2

1 165
2 5 times
3 2 hrs 28 mins

Challenge 3

1 a) 08:10
  b) 1 hr 23 mins
  c) 12 mins
  d) 25 mins
2 19 February
3 9 p.m.

Pages 48–49
Challenge 1

1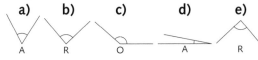
  a) b) c) d) e)
  A R O A R

2 55° (accept 53° to 57°)
3 a) EF   b) GH
4 7 cm

Challenge 2

1 15
2 **Answers could include:**

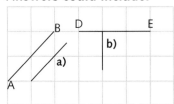

3 $x = 107°$

Challenge 3

1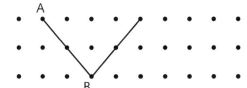
  A
  B

2 80 cm
3 a) D   b) C
4 a) $x = 45°$ b) $x = 267°$

Pages 50–51
Challenge 1

1 Trapezium   C   Rhombus   E
  Octagon   D   Pentagon   B
  Circle   A
2 $x = 80°$
3 $x = 90°$ B = 12 cm

Challenge 2

1

2 $x = 83°$ B = 8 cm
3 a) Side A = Side B ✓
  c) Angles W° + X° + Y° + Z° = 360° ✓

Challenge 3

1 a) A hexagon has six sides ✓
  b) A triangle can have two obtuse angles ✗
  c) All quadrilaterals have angles that equal 90° ✗
  d) The angles on a straight line equal 180° ✓
  e) The interior angles of an equilateral triangle
     are all 80° ✗
2 $x = 75°$

Pages 52–53
Challenge 1

1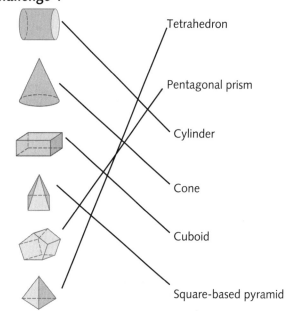
  Tetrahedron
  Pentagonal prism
  Cylinder
  Cone
  Cuboid
  Square-based pyramid

2 Cylinder

7

Answers

Challenge 2

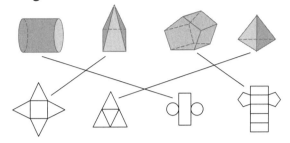

2 Answers could include:

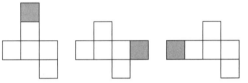

3 Cone

Challenge 3

1 Answers could include:

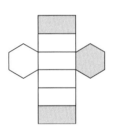

2 Octagon and Triangle

3

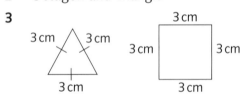

Pages 54–55
Challenge 1

1

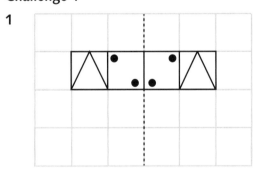

2

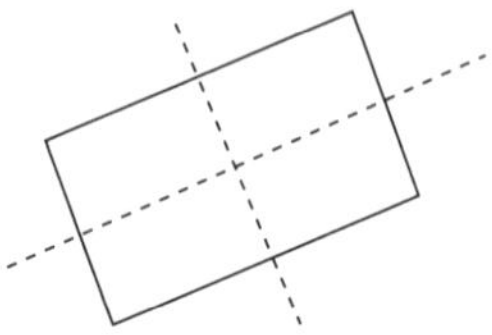

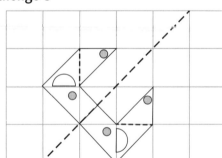

3 c)

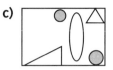

Challenge 2

1

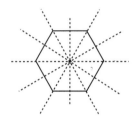

2

3 c)

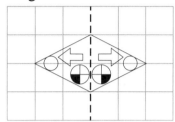

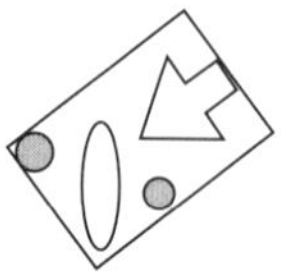

Challenge 3

1

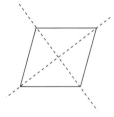

2

3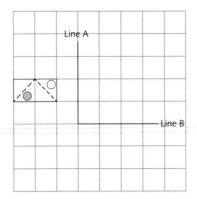

Pages 56–59
Progress Test 3
1   XCVI
2   108°
3   **a)** Bus C
    b) Bus B
    c) 37 mins
4   $\frac{1}{8}$
5   115.78
6   42 m
7   136
8   52p   £0.55   £5   £5.02   520p
9   **a)** 0.235 l   **b)** 765 ml
10 16 cm
11 44 cm
12 72 cm³
13 17.5 cm²
14 65°

15

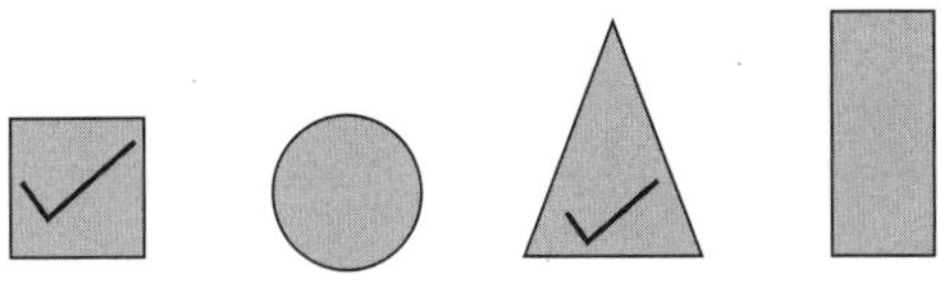

16

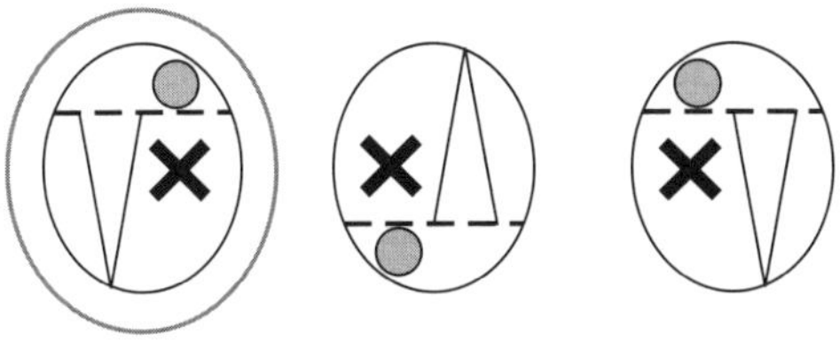

17 125
18 **a)** a and e   **b)** a and c or c and e
19 1976
20 165
21 3 km < 3200 m
    250 ml = $\frac{1}{4}$ l
    32 cm < 325 mm
    600 g > 0.5 kg

22 $\frac{1}{24}$
23 £20.03

Pages 60–61
Challenge 1
1   **a)**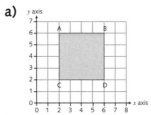
    b) Square
    c) Origin

Challenge 2
1   **a)**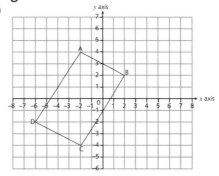
    b) Parallelogram
    c) (–4,–3)

Challenge 3
1   **a), b)**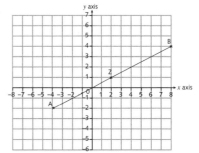
    c) (2,1)
    d) Zero

Answers

Pages 62–63
Challenge 1
1 a) (2,6) (4,6) (4,3) (2,3)

b)
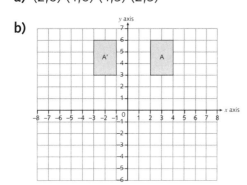

c) (–3,6) (–1,6) (–1,3) (–3,3)

Challenge 2
1 a) (1,5) (5,1) (1,1)

b)
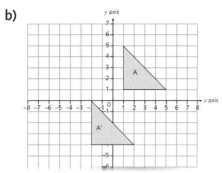

c) (2,–4) (–2,–4) (–2,0)

Challenge 3
1 a) (2,–3) (3,–5) (6,–1) (7,–3)

b)
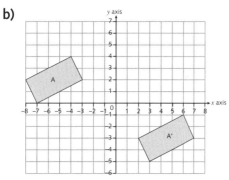

c) (–8, 2) (–7,0) (–3,2) (–4,4)

Pages 64–65
Challenge 1
1 a) (2,1) (4,1) (4,4) (2,4)

b)
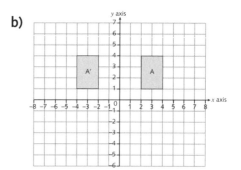

c) (–2,1) (–4,1) (–4,4) (–2,4)

Challenge 2
1 a) (–2,1) (–6,1) (–6,5)

b)
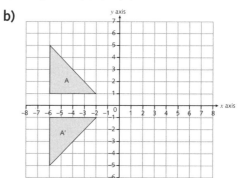

c) (–2,–1) (–6,–1) (–6,–5)
d) They are the same.

Challenge 3
1 a)
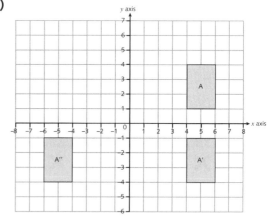

b) A (4,1) (6,1) (6,4) (4,4)
   A′ (4,–1) (6,–1) (6,–4) (4,–4)

10

Pages 66–67
Challenge 1
1 a)

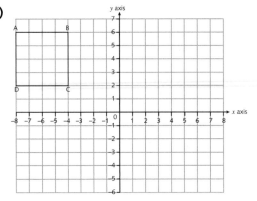

b) D (–8,2)
c) (–6,6)

Challenge 2
1 a)

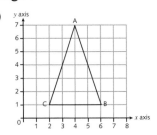

b) C (2,1)
c) (4,1)

Challenge 3
1 a) (6,8)
b) (10,8)
c) (10,6)
d) (2,6)

Pages 68–69
Challenge 1
1 a) 4 hours
b) January
2 14
3 $\frac{1}{2}$

Challenge 2
1 a) July
b) 11 hours
2 *Futurama*
3 50%

Challenge 3
1 3 months
2 10%
3 a) $\frac{1}{4}$
b) 7

Pages 70–71
Challenge 1
1 a) 2 hrs 20 mins
b) Bus A
c) Cricket Ground and Mason Road

Challenge 2
1 a) 18 mins
b) 47 mins
2 10

Challenge 3
1 a) 1945
b) 47 mins
2 7

Pages 72–73
Challenge 1
1

2 1:2   1:3   1:4   1:4

3 Answers could include:

a)   b)   c)

2 black : 3 white   1 black : 2 white   2 black : 3 white : 1 grey

Answers

Challenge 2
1 No. (You would need 3 more black to fit the 2:3 ratio (need 12 white:18 black))
2 1:3 — 5:5
   1:1 — 6:15
   16:24 — 2:3
   8:32 — 9:27
   2:5 — 1:4
3 Flour   300 g
   Sugar   180 g
   Butter   360 g
   Eggs   3
4 2.5 times

Challenge 3
1 a) 12 bananas, 6 oranges
   b) 24 bananas, 36 apples and 12 oranges
2 Sam has 39:52 = 3:4 (blue:red)
3 15 cm and 45 cm

Pages 74–75
Challenge 1
1 $x = 7$
2 3 6 9 **12 15 18**
3 $y = 27$
4 $x = 8$
5 25
6 $x = 3$
7 1,4; 2,3; 3,2; 4,1; 0,5; 5,0
8

n	$3n + 2$
1	5
5	17
10	32
20	62
100	302

Challenge 2
1 $x = 5$
2 Add 5 each time
3 $y = 3$
4 1,12; 2,6; 3,4; 12,1; 6,2; 4,3

5 21
6 13   7   1   **–5   –11   –17**
7 $a = 11$ $b = 4$

Challenge 3
1 Doubles each time
2 $a = 28$
3 1,24; 2,12; 3,8; 4,6; 24,1; 12,2; 8,3; 6,4
4 3   9   21   45   **93**
5

n	$2n + 5$	$3n$	$100n$
5	15	15	500
15	35	45	1500
10	25	30	1000
0.6	6.2	1.8	60

Pages 76–80
Progress Test 4
1 a) b) d)

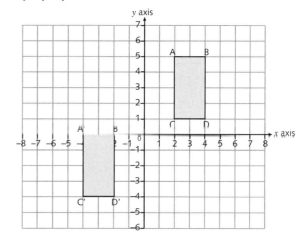

c) D(4,1)
e) A'(–4,0) B'(–2,0) C'(–4,–4) D'(–2,–4)
2 a) 60%   b) 28%   c) 20%
3 10
4 3
5

For 4 people	
Beef	48 g
Tomato sauce	40 g
Onions	20 g

6

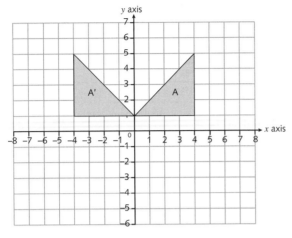

(−4,5) (−4,1) (0,1)

7 15

8 8 : 23 ⟨12 : 45⟩ 8 : 35 12 : 30

9 2,7 or 7,2

10 $a = 8$

11

n	$5n$	$4n - 3$
6	30	21
10	50	37
9	45	33

12 a) millimetres (mm)
   b) 7
   c) 5
   d) 102 mm
   e) 12 mm

13 $\frac{1}{20}$

14 a) Bus A
   b) Bus C
   c) Bus C
   d) Bus C

15 B(4,7) C(0,7) D(0,3)

16

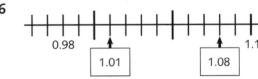

17 37°C

18 76 000

19 60°

20 75 cm^2

21 125 cm^3

22 Triangular-based prism

23 5.20 p.m.

Progress Test Charts

Progress Test 1

Q	Topic	✓ or ✗	See page
1	Roman Numerals		9
2	More Mental Addition and Subtraction		12
3	Place Value		4
4	Place Value		4
5	Negative Numbers		6
6	Number Facts for Mental Calculations		10
7	More Mental Addition and Subtraction		12
8	Number Facts for Mental Calculations		10
9	Roman Numerals		9
10	Place Value		4
11	Number Facts for Mental Calculations		10
12	More Mental Addition and Subtraction		12
13	Written Addition and Subtraction		14
14	Place Value		4
15	Rounding		8
16	Written Addition and Subtraction		14
17	Number Facts for Mental Calculations		10
18	Place Value		4
19	Roman Numerals		9
20	Number Facts for Mental Calculations		10
21	More Mental Addition and Subtraction		12
22	Negative Numbers		6
23	Number Facts for Mental Calculations		10
24	Place Value		4
25	Written Addition and Subtraction		14
26	Negative Numbers		6
27	Negative Numbers		6
28	More Mental Addition and Subtraction		12
29	More Mental Addition and Subtraction		12
30	Written Addition and Subtraction		14
31	Written Addition and Subtraction		14

Progress Test 2

Q	Topic	✓ or ✗	See page
1	Prime, Square and Cube Numbers		22
2	Adding, Subtracting, Multiplying and Dividing Fractions		32
3	All Kinds of Numbers		20
4	Adding, Subtracting, Multiplying and Dividing Fractions		32
5	Written Addition and Subtraction		14
6	All Kinds of Numbers		20
7	Improper Fractions and Mixed Numbers		34
8	Percentages		35
9	Prime, Square and Cube Numbers		22
10	Place Value		4
11	Prime, Square and Cube Numbers		22
12	Adding, Subtracting, Multiplying and Dividing Fractions		32
13	Improper Fractions and Mixed Numbers		34
14	Prime, Square and Cube Numbers		22
15	Short and Long Division		28
16	Adding, Subtracting, Multiplying and Dividing Fractions		32
17	Percentages		35
18	All Kinds of Numbers		20
19	Negative Numbers		6
20	Written Multiplication		26
21	Rounding		8
22	Percentages		35
23	Roman Numerals		9
24	Multiplying and Dividing		24
25	Number Facts for Mental Calculations		10
26	Prime, Square and Cube Numbers		22
27	Decimal Fractions		33
28	Short and Long Division		28
29	More Mental Addition and Subtraction		12
30	Fractions		30
31	Fractions		30
32	Rounding		8
33	Multiplying and Dividing		24
34	Prime, Square and Cube Numbers		22
35	All Kinds of Numbers		20
36	Percentages		35
37	Multiplying and Dividing		24

Progress Test 3

Q	Topic	✓ or X	See page
1	Roman Numerals		9
2	Angles, Lines and Circles		48
3	Time		46
4	Adding, Subtracting, Multiplying and Dividing Fractions		32
5	Written Multiplication		26
6	Perimeter and Area		42
7	Percentages		35
8	Place Value		4
9	Units of Measurement		40
10	Angles, Lines and Circles		48
11	Perimeter and Area, 2-D Shapes		42, 50
12	Area, Volume and Money		44
13	Area, Volume and Money		44
14	Angles, Lines and Circles		48
15	3-D Shapes and Nets		52
16	Symmetry		54
17	Prime, Square and Cube Numbers		22
18	Angles, Lines and Circles		48
19	Written Multiplication		26
20	Number Facts for Mental Calculations		10
21	Units of Measurement		40
22	Adding, Subtracting, Multiplying and Dividing Fractions		32
23	More Mental Addition and Subtraction		12

Progress Test 4

Q	Topic	✓ or X	See page
1	Plotting Points, Translation, Missing Coordinates		60, 62, 66
2	Percentages		35
3	Timetables and Calculating the Mean		70
4	Timetables and Calculating the Mean		70
5	Ratio and Proportion		72
6	Reflection		64
7	Prime, Square and Cube Numbers		22
8	Ratio and Proportion		72
9	Prime, Square and Cube Numbers, Solving Equations		22, 74
10	Solving Equations		74
11	Solving Equations		74
12	All Types of Charts, Timetables and Calculating the Mean		68, 70
13	Adding, Subtracting, Multiplying and Dividing Fractions		32
14	Timetables and Calculating the Mean		70
15	Missing Coordinates		66
16	Place Value		4
17	Negative Numbers		6
18	Rounding		8
19	Angles, Lines and Circles		48
20	Perimeter and Area		42
21	Area, Volume and Money		44
22	3-D Shapes and Nets		52
23	Time		46

What am I doing well in? _____

_____

What do I need to improve? _____

_____

Notes

Units of Measurement

PS **3** Jared runs 367 m. How much further does he need to run to reach 1 km?

_____ m

1 mark

PS **4** Maya puts four apples on the scales shown. How much does one apple weigh?

_____ g

1 mark

Marks.......... /9

Challenge 3

PS **1** A school nurse measures the children's height. Vic is $1\frac{1}{2}$ m tall and Bob is 1.3 m tall.

How much taller is Vic than Bob in cm? _____ cm

1 mark

2 Match the letters on the scale to the measurements below.

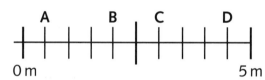

0 m   5 m

| 2 m | _____ |
| 0.5 m | _____ |

| $4\frac{1}{2}$m | _____ |
| 300 cm | _____ |

4 marks

3 Circle the metric measurements to the nearest imperial equivalent. The first one has been done for you.

a) **1 pint**   50 ml   (500 ml)   5 l

b) **5 miles**   8 m   80 km   8 km

c) **4 inches**   1 cm   100 cm   10 cm

2 marks

Marks.......... /7

Total marks .... /25   How am I doing?

Perimeter and Area

PS Problem-solving questions

Challenge 1

1 Work out the perimeter of this rectangle.

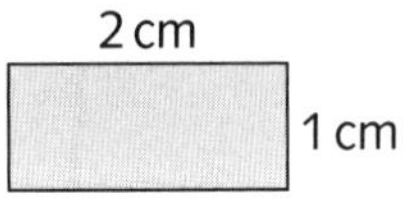

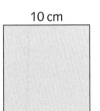

2 cm
1 cm

P = ______ cm

1 mark

2 Calculate the perimeter of this shape.

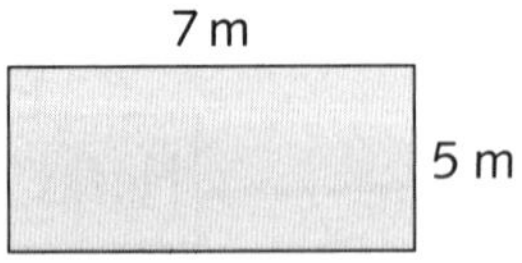

7 m
5 m

P = ______ m

1 mark

3 What is the area of the square?

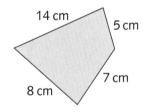

10 cm

A = ______ cm^2

1 mark

Marks........../3

Challenge 2

1 Calculate the perimeter of the shape.

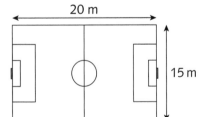

14 cm
5 cm
7 cm
8 cm

P = ______ cm

1 mark

2 What is the area of the football pitch?

20 m
15 m

A = ______ m^2

1 mark

Perimeter and Area

PS **3** What is the perimeter of the penguin enclosure?

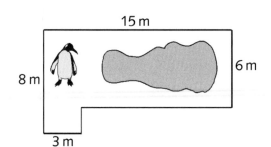

15 m

8 m

6 m

3 m

P = _____ m

1 mark

Marks............/3

Challenge 3

PS **1** This is Farmer Smith's hen enclosure.

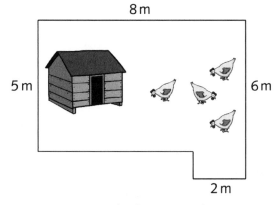

8 m

5 m

6 m

2 m

a) How much fencing does Farmer Smith need to buy to go around his hen enclosure?

1 mark

b) What is the area of the enclosure?

_____

1 mark

PS **2** The area of a rectangle is 35 cm².
What could the lengths of the sides be in cm?

_____ cm and _____ cm

2 marks

Marks.........../4

Total marks ..../10   How am I doing?

Area, Volume and Money

PS Problem-solving questions

Challenge 1

1 Calculate the area of this triangle.

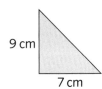

9 cm
7 cm

A = ________ cm^2

1 mark

2 Order these amounts from smallest to biggest.

501p 51p £5 551p 5p

____

1 mark

3 Calculate the volume of this cube.

1 cm
1 cm

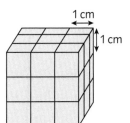

V = ________ cm^3

1 mark

Marks........../3

Challenge 2

1 What is the area of this parallelogram?

5 cm
8 cm

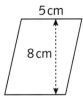

A = ________ cm^2

1 mark

2 What is the volume of this shape?

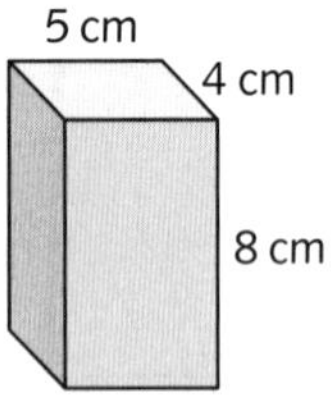

5 cm
4 cm
8 cm

V = ________ cm^3

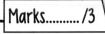

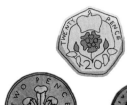

1 mark

PS **3** Using only coins of these values, how can you make 37p using the least number of coins?

TWENTY PENCE
20
TWO PENCE
2
5

____

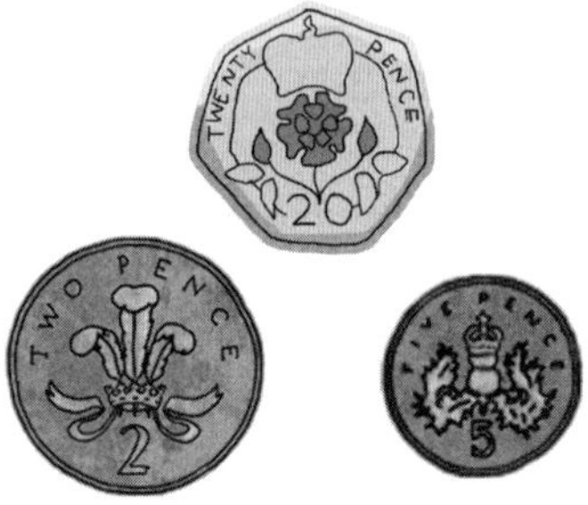

1 mark

Marks........../3

Area, Volume and Money

Challenge 3

PS **1** A cube has a volume of 27 cm³.

What are the lengths of its sides?

_____ cm

2 What is the area of this shape?

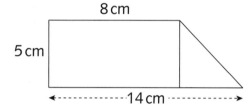

A = _____ cm²

PS **3** Ben has some money. If he rounds it to the nearest 10p and then multiplies it by 10, he has £4.00.

How much money could he have had to start with?

_____

PS **4** How much water in cm³ can this container hold?

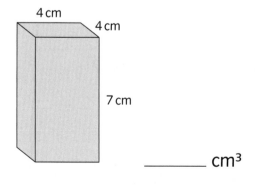

_____ cm³

Marks.......... /4

Total marks .... /10   How am I doing?

Time

Challenge 1

1 Complete the blanks.

a) A clock face shows _____ hours. There are _____ hours in one day.

b) Each hour is _____ minutes long. Two minutes equals _____ seconds.

c) There are usually _____ days in a year. June has _____ days.

6 marks

PS **2** Jonny leaves home at the time shown here every morning.
He gets to school 25 minutes later.
What time does he get to school?

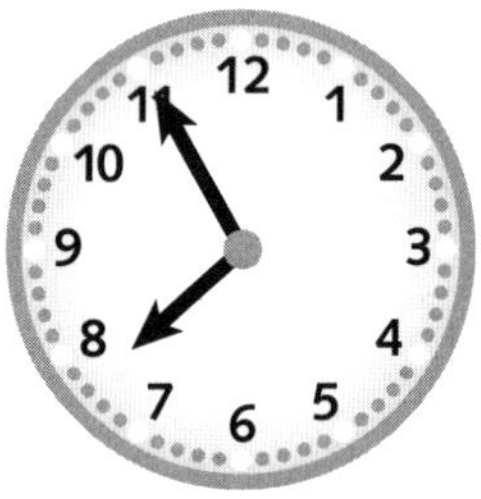

_____

1 mark

PS **3** Lena puts a cake in the oven at 4.50 p.m. It bakes for $1\frac{1}{2}$ hours. What time does Lena take her cake out of the oven?

_____

1 mark

Marks.......... /8

Challenge 2

PS **1** Emily completes a puzzle in $2\frac{1}{2}$ minutes.

Olivia takes 15 seconds longer.

How long did Olivia take in seconds? _____

1 mark

PS **2** Freddie goes to karate every Monday night. If 1 September is a Monday, how many times does he go to karate in September?

_____

1 mark

PS **3** Both clocks show morning times.
What is the time difference between the two clocks in hours and minutes?

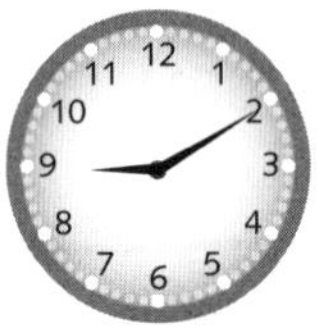

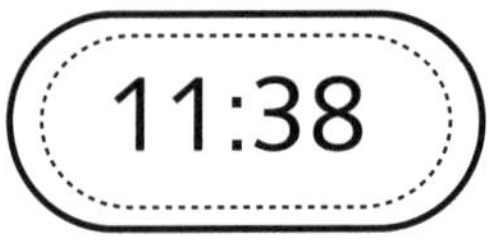

11:38

_____

2 marks

Marks.......... /4

46

Challenge 3

PS **1** Look at the train timetable below.

Crewe	08:10	10:20	11:15	–	15:05
Wilmslow	08:55	10:48	–	13:40	15:55
Manchester	09:33	–	12:20	14:10	16:15

a) Annie is meeting a friend in Manchester for lunch at 12:00 noon.

What train will she need to catch at Crewe? _____

1 mark

b) How long does it take the first train to travel from Crewe to Manchester?

_____

1 mark

c) Bill gets to Wilmslow station at 11:00. How many minutes was he late for the train that just left?

_____

1 mark

d) Jenny arrives at Crewe station at 10:50. How long will she have to wait for the next train?

_____

1 mark

PS **2** Natasha came back from a fortnight's holiday on 4 March. What date did she go away if it was a leap year?

_____

1 mark

PS **3** Brian starts his homework and works for $1\frac{1}{2}$ hours. He then has a quarter of an hour break before completing his homework for another 50 minutes.

If he started work after his tea at 6.25 p.m., when did he finish his homework?

_____

1 mark

Marks.......... /6

Total marks .... /18   How am I doing?

47

Angles, Lines and Circles

Challenge 1

1 Label the angles A = Acute, O = Obtuse and R = Right angle. The first one has been done for you.

a) b) c) d) e)

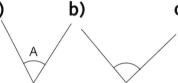

A

4 marks

2 Use a protractor to measure this angle.

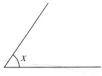

x $x =$ _____ °

1 mark

3 Look at the lines below. Which line is:

a) parallel to line AB? _____

b) perpendicular to line AB? _____

B

G

C ——— D

F

A

H

E

2 marks

4 What is the diameter of a circle if the radius is 3.5 cm? _____

1 mark

Marks.......... /8

Challenge 2

1 Amelia's bracelet is made with beads with a diameter of 2 cm.

If her bracelet measures 30 cm, how many beads are on it? _____

1 mark

2 a) Draw a line parallel to line AB.

b) Draw a line perpendicular to line DE.

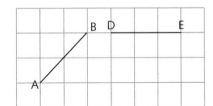

B D   E

A

2 marks

3 Work out angle x. $x =$ _____ °

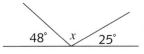

48° x 25°

1 mark

Marks.......... /4

48

Angles, Lines and Circles

Challenge 3

1 Draw a line from point B to another dot to make a right angle at B.

1 mark

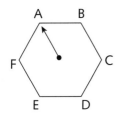

PS **2** My pattern has 16 circles side by side. If the radius of each circle is 2.5 cm, how long is my pattern?

____

1 mark

PS **3** This shape is a regular hexagon.

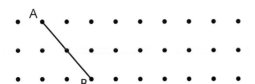

a) If the pointer is turned 180° from point A, which letter is it pointing at now?

______

1 mark

b) If I turn the pointer 120° clockwise from A, which letter is it pointing at now?

______

1 mark

4 What is angle x in the diagrams below?

a)

$x =$ ______ °

b)

$x =$ ______ °

2 marks

Marks........./6

Total marks ..../18 How am I doing?

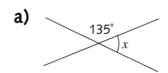

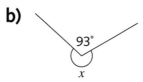

2-D Shapes

Challenge 1

1 Match the names to the shapes.

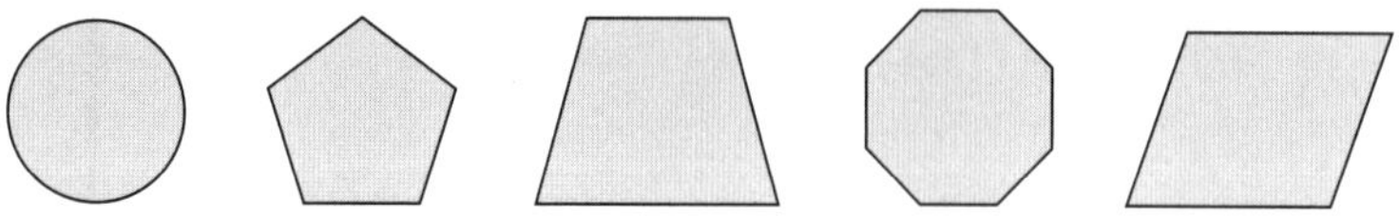

A   **B**   **C**   **D**   **E**

Trapezium   _____   Rhombus   _____

Octagon   _____   Pentagon   _____

Circle   _____

5 marks

2 Work out angle x.

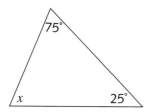

$x = $ _____ °

1 mark

3 Find angle x and the length of side B.

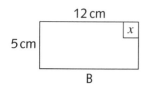

$x = $ _____ °   B = _____ cm

2 marks

Marks.......... /8

Challenge 2

1 Circle the isosceles triangles:

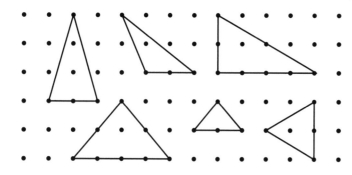

3 marks

50

2-D Shapes

2 Find angle x and the length of side B. The opposite sides are equal length and are parallel.

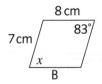

$x =$ _____ $^\circ$

$B =$ _____ cm

2 marks

3 Look at this shape. It is **not** drawn to scale. Opposite sides are equal length. Tick the statements which are correct:

a) Side A = Side B

b) Side B is perpendicular to side D

c) Angles W° + X° + Y° + Z° = 360°

d) Side C is parallel to side A

2 marks

Marks.......... /7

Challenge 3

1 Put a tick (✓) if the statement is true and a cross (✗) if the statement is false:

a) A hexagon has six sides

b) A triangle can have two obtuse angles

c) All quadrilaterals have angles that equal 90°

d) The angles on a straight line equal 180°

e) The interior angles of an equilateral triangle are all 80°

5 marks

PS **2** Work out angle x.

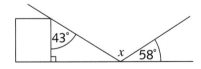

$x =$ _____ $^\circ$

1 mark

Marks.......... /6

Total marks .... /21   How am I doing?

3-D Shapes and Nets

PS Problem-solving questions

Challenge 1

1 Draw lines to match the names to the shapes.

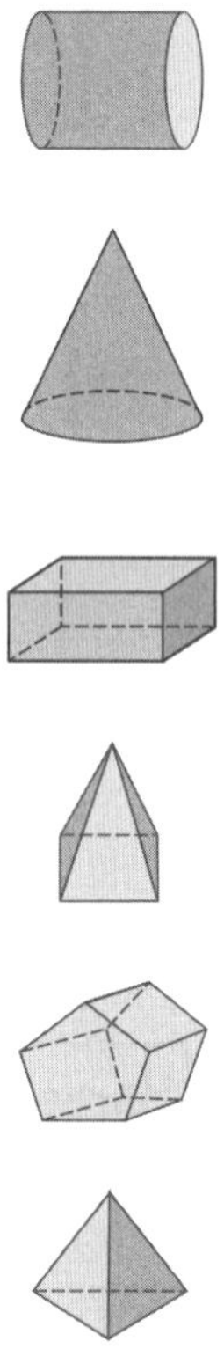

Tetrahedron

Pentagonal prism

Cylinder

Cone

Cuboid

Square-based pyramid

5 marks

2 What shape will this net make?

_____

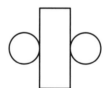

1 mark

Marks.......... /6

Challenge 2

1 Draw lines to match the nets to the shapes.

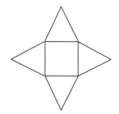

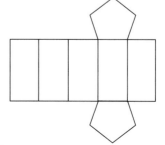

3 marks

3-D Shapes and Nets

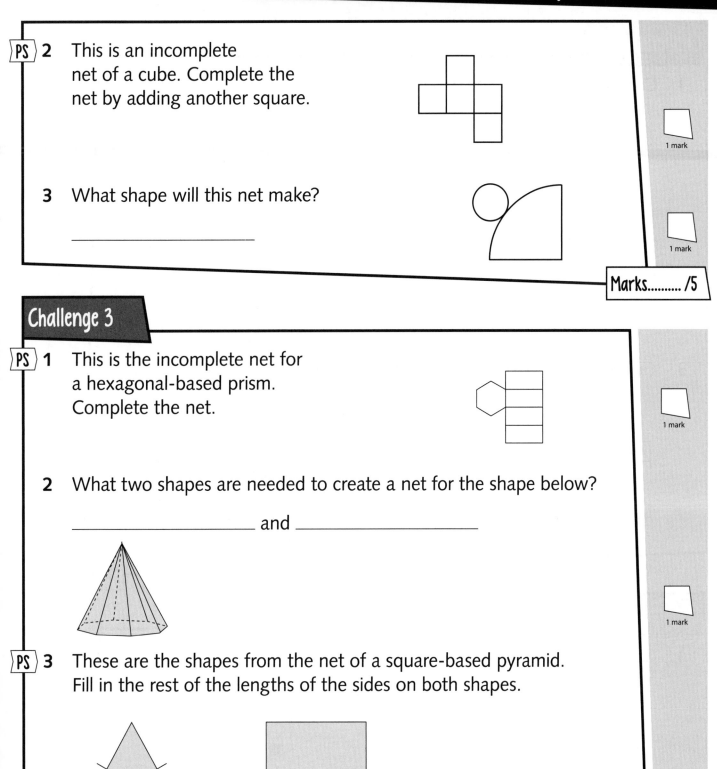

PS 2 This is an incomplete
net of a cube. Complete the
net by adding another square.

1 mark

3 What shape will this net make?

_____

1 mark

Marks.......... /5

Challenge 3

PS 1 This is the incomplete net for
a hexagonal-based prism.
Complete the net.

1 mark

2 What two shapes are needed to create a net for the shape below?

_____ and _____

1 mark

PS 3 These are the shapes from the net of a square-based pyramid.
Fill in the rest of the lengths of the sides on both shapes.

3 cm

2 marks

Marks.......... /4

Total marks .... /15   How am I doing?

53

Symmetry

Challenge 1

1 Complete the pattern to make it symmetrical.

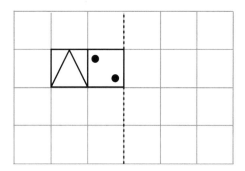

2 marks

2 Draw the lines of symmetry for this shape.

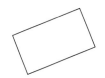

1 mark

3 Tick the correct pattern after reflection in the line of symmetry.

a) ☐   b) ☐   c) ☐

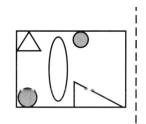      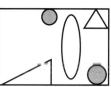   

1 mark

Marks.......... /4

Challenge 2

1 Complete the pattern to make it symmetrical.

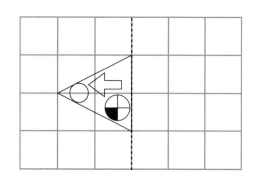

3 marks

2 Draw the lines of symmetry for this shape.

1 mark

Symmetry

3 Tick the correct pattern after reflection in the line of symmetry.

a) b) c)

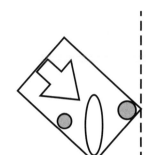 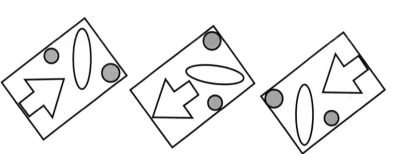

1 mark

Marks.......... /5

Challenge 3

1 Complete the pattern to make it symmetrical.

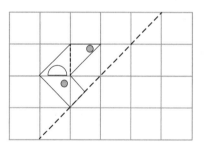

3 marks

2 Draw the lines of symmetry for this shape.

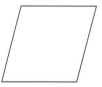

1 mark

PS 3 This shape has been reflected in line of symmetry A and then line B. The finished shape is shown. Draw the original shape.

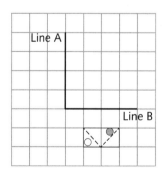

2 marks

Marks.......... /6

Total marks .... /15   How am I doing?

Progress Test 3

PS⟩ **1** Work out this calculation and write your answer in Roman numerals:

XLIV + LII = _____

⬜ 1 mark

PS⟩ **2** Work out angle *x*.

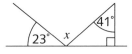

x = _____°

⬜ 1 mark

PS⟩ **3** Look at this bus timetable.

	Bus A	Bus B	Bus C
Claude's Corner	09:20	11:18	12:05
Wild Boar Bend	11:45	13:52	14:20
Flat Rock	15:35	16:55	17:38

a) Which bus gets from Claude's Corner to Flat Rock the quickest?

_____

⬜ 1 mark

b) Beau is meeting his friends at Wild Boar Bend at 2 p.m.

Which is the latest bus he could catch? _____

⬜ 1 mark

c) Enid gets to Claude's Corner at 11:55. How late was she for Bus B?

_____

⬜ 1 mark

4 $\frac{3}{8} + \frac{2}{8} - \frac{4}{8} = $ ☐

⬜ 1 mark

5
```
  1 6.5 4
×       7
_____
```

⬜ 1 mark

6 Calculate the perimeter of Farmer Biggs' field.

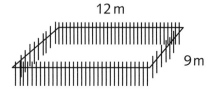

12 m

9 m

P = _____

⬜ 1 mark

56

7 Find 85% of 160. ______________ 1 mark

8 Order these amounts from smallest to largest.

52p £5 £5.02 520p £0.55

____ 1 mark

PS 9 Peter pours 235 ml of squash into a jug.

a) How many litres is this? ______________ 1 mark

b) He fills the jug up to the 1 litre mark.

How much more liquid has he added? ______________ ml 1 mark

10 What is the length of the radius of my circle?

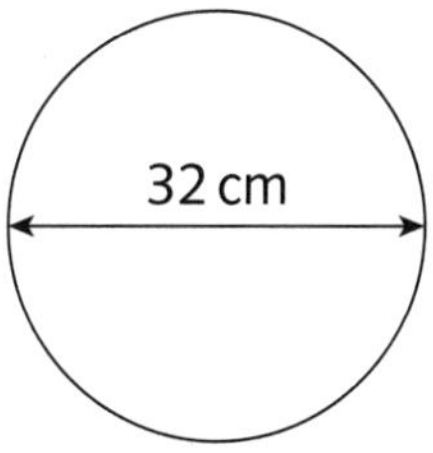
32 cm

______________ 1 mark

PS 11 Each side of a regular octagon measures 5.5 cm.

What is the perimeter of the shape? P = ______________ cm 1 mark

12 What is the volume of this cuboid?

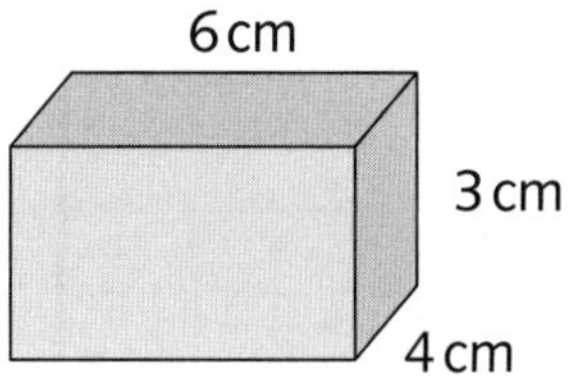
6 cm
3 cm
4 cm

V = ______________ cm^3 1 mark

13 Calculate the area of this triangle.

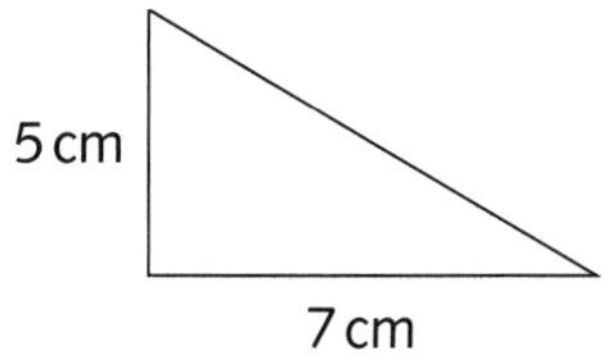
5 cm
7 cm

A = ______________ cm^2 1 mark

14 What is angle x?

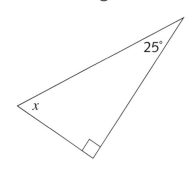

25°

x

$x =$ _____ °

15 Tick the 2-D shapes required to make this 3-D shape.

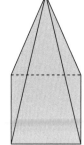

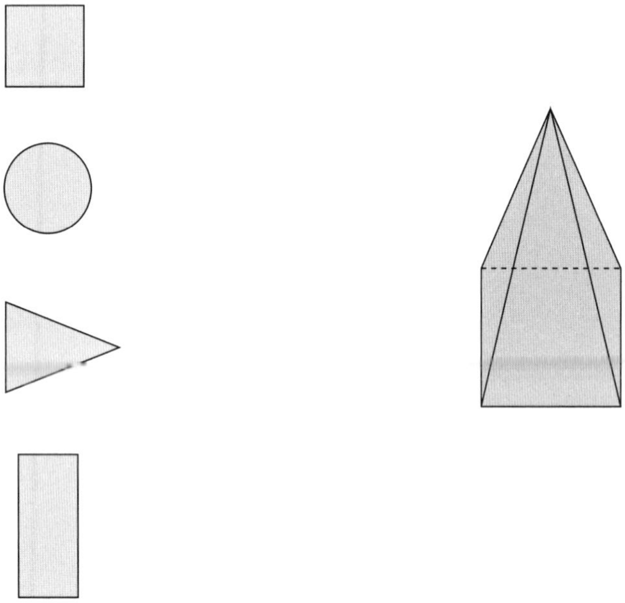

16 Circle the shape which is the reflected image of the first one.

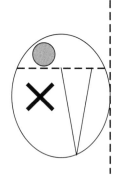
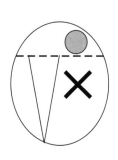
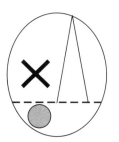
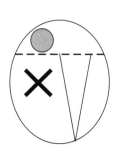

17 $5^3 =$ _____

18 Look at the lines below.

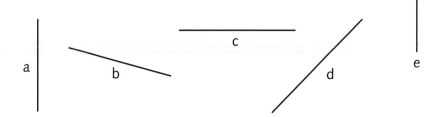

a) Which two lines are parallel to each other? _____ and _____

1 mark

b) Find two lines which are perpendicular to each other.

_____ and _____

1 mark

19   2 4 7

    ×   8

    _____

1 mark

20 A concert hall has 1100 seats.

If 935 people attend a performance, how many seats are left empty in the hall?

_____

1 mark

21 Use >, < and = to make these statements correct.

3 km ☐ 3200 m   32 cm ☐ 325 mm

250 ml ☐ $\frac{1}{4}$ l   600 g ☐ 0.5 kg

4 marks

22 $\frac{1}{12} ÷ 2 =$ ☐

1 mark

PS **23** Jo-Shun buys these items from a sports shop:

Tracksuit: £29.99   Trainers: £39.99   Cap: £9.99

How much change does he get from £100? £ _____

1 mark

Marks........ /30

Plotting Points

1 a) Plot these points on the grid.

A(2,6)

B(6,6)

C(2,2)

D(6,2)

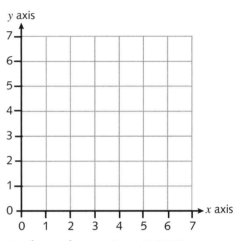

b) Join the points with straight lines. What shape is ABCD?

_____

c) What is point (0,0) called? _____

4 marks

1 mark

1 mark

Marks.......... /6

1 a) Plot these points on the grid. A(–2,4) B(2,2) C(–2,–4) D(–6,–2)

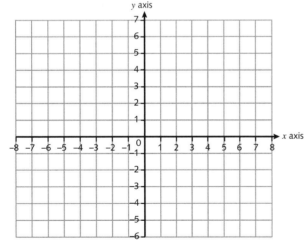

b) Join the points with straight lines. What shape is ABCD?

_____

c) Find the point half way along line CD. What are its coordinates?

_____

4 marks

1 mark

1 mark

Marks.......... /6

Plotting Points

Challenge 3

1 a) Plot these points on the grid and join them with a straight line.

A(–4,–2)

B(8,4)

2 marks

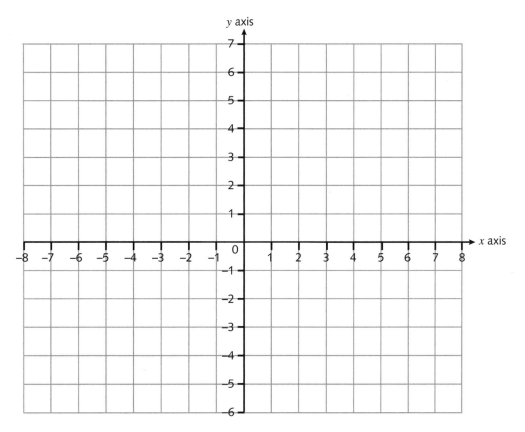

b) Point Z is the midpoint of the line AB. Plot point Z.

1 mark

c) What are the coordinates of point Z? ____________

1 mark

d) What are the *x* coordinates of every point on the *y* axis?

____

1 mark

Marks........../5

Total marks ..../17 How am I doing?

Translation

PS Problem-solving questions

Challenge 1

1

a) What are the coordinates of the vertices of shape A? 4 marks

____

b) Translate shape A 5 squares left to become shape A′. 4 marks

c) Give the coordinates of A′. ______________________ 4 marks

Marks........./12

Challenge 2

1

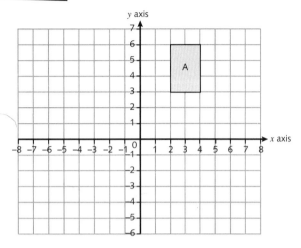

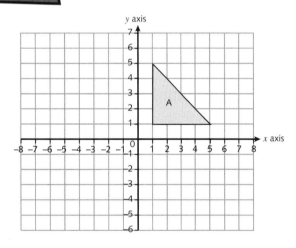

a) What are the coordinates of the vertices of shape A? 3 marks

____

b) Translate shape A 3 squares left and 5 squares down to become shape A′. 3 marks

c) Give the coordinates of A′. ______________________ 3 marks

Marks........../9

Translation

Challenge 3

PS **1**

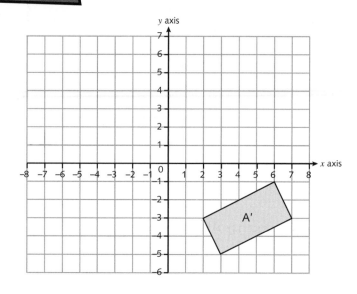

a) Give the coordinates of the vertices of shape A'.

_____

4 marks

b) Shape A' is the result of the translation of shape A. Shape A was translated 10 squares right and 5 squares down to produce shape A'.

Draw shape A on the grid.

4 marks

c) Give the coordinates of shape A.

_____

4 marks

Marks.........../12

Total marks ..../33   How am I doing? 😊 😐 😣

Reflection

PS Problem-solving questions

Challenge 1

1 a) Give the coordinates of shape A.

____

____

____

____

4 marks

b) Reflect shape A in the y axis to give shape A′. Draw shape A′.

4 marks

c) Give the coordinates for shape A′.

____

1 mark

Marks........../9

Challenge 2

1 a) Give the coordinates of shape A.

____

____

____

3 marks

b) Reflect shape A in the x axis to give shape A′. Draw shape A′.

3 marks

c) Give the coordinates for shape A′.

____

3 marks

d) What do you notice about the x coordinates of both shapes?

____

1 mark

Marks........./10

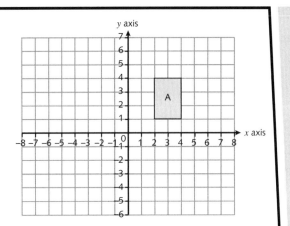

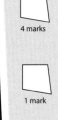

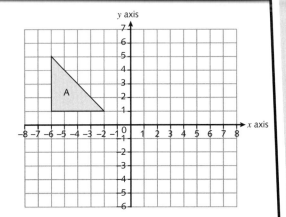

Reflection

Challenge 3

PS **1** Shape A was reflected in the *x* axis to give shape A'.

Shape A' was then reflected in the *y* axis to produce shape A''.

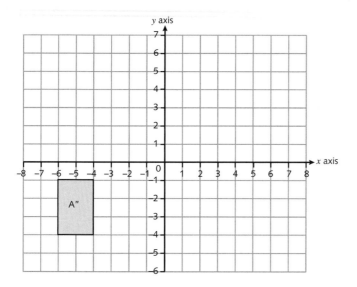

a) Plot and draw shapes A and A'.

b) Give the coordinates for shapes A and A'.

_____

_____

2 marks

8 marks

Marks......... /10

Total marks .... /29   How am I doing?

Missing Coordinates

PS Problem-solving questions

Challenge 1

1 a) Shape ABCD is a square. Plot point D and draw straight lines to complete the shape.

2 marks

b) Give the coordinates for point D. ______________________

1 mark

c) What are the coordinates of the point half way between A and B?

____

1 mark

Marks........../4

Challenge 2

PS 1 a) Shape ABC is an isosceles triangle with BC being the shortest side. Plot point C and draw straight lines to complete the shape.

2 marks

b) Give the coordinates for point C. ______________________

1 mark

c) What are the coordinates of the point half way between B and C?

____

1 mark

Marks........../4

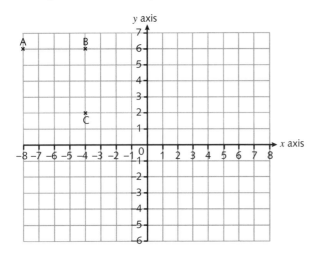

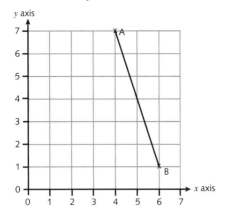

Missing Coordinates

Challenge 3

PS **1** Shapes A and B are identical rectangles where the length of each rectangle is double the width of the rectangle (ab is double the length of bc).

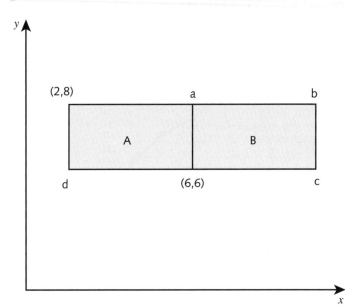

Give the coordinates of points a, b, c and d.

a) a = _____

b) b = _____

c) c = _____

d) d = _____

4 marks

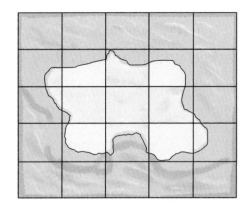

Marks.......... /4

Total marks .... /12   How am I doing?

All Types of Charts

Look at these charts and then answer the questions.

Scientists measured the number of hours of sunshine each month across the UK. They put the information into a chart:

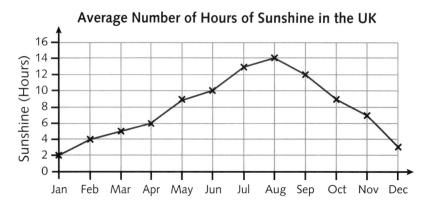

Average Number of Hours of Sunshine in the UK

One hundred children were surveyed about their favourite TV shows:

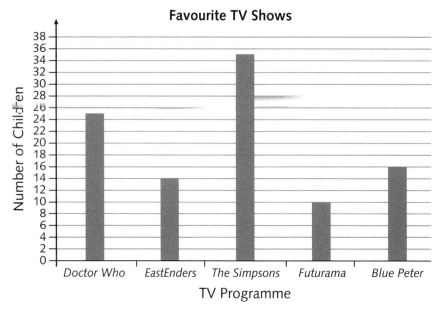

Favourite TV Shows

Forty children in Year 6 were asked which animals they kept as pets:

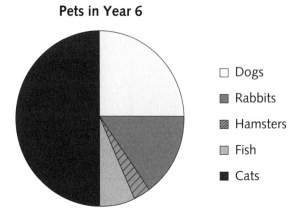

Pets in Year 6

☐ Dogs
▦ Rabbits
▨ Hamsters
▢ Fish
■ Cats

All Types of Charts

Challenge 1

1 a) How many more hours of sunshine were there in June than in April?

_____

1 mark

   b) Which month had the least sunshine? _____

1 mark

2 How many children liked *EastEnders* best? _____

1 mark

3 What fraction of Year 6 children kept cats? ☐

1 mark

Marks.......... /4

Challenge 2

1 a) Which month had the second most sunshine? _____

1 mark

   b) How much sunnier was it in August than December? _____

1 mark

2 Which was the least popular show? _____

1 mark

3 What percentage of Year 6 children kept cats? _____

1 mark

Marks.......... /4

Challenge 3

1 For how many months were there **more than** 10 hours of sunshine?

_____

1 mark

2 What percentage of children liked *Futurama* best? _____

1 mark

3 a) Estimate what fraction of Year 6 children kept dogs. ☐

1 mark

   b) If two children kept fish, estimate how many children had rabbits as pets.

_____

1 mark

Marks.......... /4

Total marks .... /12   How am I doing?   ☺ 😐 ☹

Timetables and Calculating the Mean

Challenge 1

PS ⟩ **1** Here is part of a bus timetable:

	Hill Top Road	Cricket Ground	Mason Road	Moore Corner
Bus A	08:20	09:35	10:15	11:55
Bus B	09:05	10:30	11:25	12:40

a) How long does it take Bus A to get from the Cricket Ground to Moore Corner?

_____

1 mark

b) Sheena needs to get to Mason Road to meet her friend at 11:15.

Which bus should she catch? _____

1 mark

c) Kevin was on Bus A for 40 minutes. Which two stops did he travel between?

_____

1 mark

Marks.........../3

Challenge 2

PS ⟩ **1** Here is part of a bus timetable:

MAPLE TERRACE	0829	0929	1029	1129	1229	----
North View Terrace	0832	0932	1032	1132	1232	----
Aberaman, Plough Inn	0836	0936	1036	1136	1236	----
ABERDARE, Bus Station arr	0840	0940	1040	1140	1240	----
ABERDARE, Bus Station dep	0840	0940	1040	1140	----	1340
Tesco	0845	0945	1045	1145	----	1345
Via By-pass	----	----	----	----	----	----
Rail Station	0847	0947	1047	1147	----	1347
Robertstown	0849	0949	1049	1149	----	1349

a) How long does it take the 9:29 bus to travel from Maple Terrace to the Rail Station?

_____

1 mark

b) Hassan arrives at Tesco at 10:58. How long will he wait for the next bus?

_____

1 mark

Timetables and Calculating the Mean

2 Calculate the mean for this set of data.

12   9   15   6   7   11

_____

1 mark

Marks............/3

Challenge 3

1 This is part of a train timetable:

London Paddington	d	1903	1915	1930	2000	2030	2100	2130	2200	2215
Reading	d	1935	1945	2003	2030	2100	2130	2200	2230	2245
Didcot Parkway	d	1949	–	2017	2044	2114	2144	2214	2244	2259
Swindon	d	2009	2015	2036	2103	2133	2203	2233	2303	2319
Kamble	a	2022	–	–	–	–	–	2250	–	–
Stroud	a	2037	–	–	–	–	–	2305	–	–
Stonehouse	a	2042	–	–	–	–	–	2310	–	–
Gloucester	a	2053	–	–	–	–	–	2323	–	–
Cheltenham Spa	a	2108	–	–	–	–	–	2335	–	–
Chippenham	a	–	–	2049	–	2145	–	2345	–	2332

a) Which is the latest train Ava could catch from Reading to meet a friend for dinner in Swindon at 8.30 p.m.?

_____

1 mark

b) How long does it take the 22:45 train from Reading to reach Chippenham?

_____

1 mark

2 The mean of a set of six numbers is 8. Five of the numbers are shown below. What is the missing sixth number?

5   9   11   6   10   _____

1 mark

Marks............/3

Total marks ..../9   How am I doing?

Ratio and Proportion

PS Problem-solving questions

Challenge 1

1 Here is a necklace. Shade the beads in the ratio of 2 white : 3 black.

1 mark

2 Simplify these ratios.

  4:8 _____   8:24 _____ 3:12 _____   4:16 _____

4 marks

3 Shade the marbles in the correct ratios.

   a)   **b)**   **c)**

     2 black : 3 white   1 black : 2 white   2 black : 3 white : 1 grey

3 marks

Marks.......... /8

Challenge 2

1 I have 12 white beads and 15 black beads. Can I make a necklace in the ratio of 2 white : 3 black and use all the beads? _____

1 mark

2 Match these ratios to their equivalents. One has been done for you.

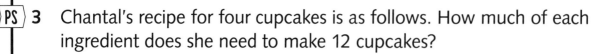

1:3   5:5

1:1   6:15

16:24   2:3

8:32   9:27

2:5   1:4

4 marks

PS 3 Chantal's recipe for four cupcakes is as follows. How much of each ingredient does she need to make 12 cupcakes?

Flour   100 g _____

Sugar   60 g _____

Butter   120 g _____

Eggs   1 _____

4 marks

Ratio and Proportion

4 How many times longer is line B than line A? _____

A _____

B _____

1 mark

Marks......... /10

Challenge 3

PS **1** Harry's smoothie recipe says he needs bananas, apples and oranges in the ratio of 2 : 3 : 1.

a) If he uses 18 apples, how many bananas and oranges does he need?

Bananas: _____

Oranges: _____

2 marks

b) If he has used 72 pieces of fruit altogether, how many of each type has he used?

Bananas: _____

Apples: _____

Oranges: _____

3 marks

PS **2** Jo has 33 blue marbles and 42 red ones. Sam has 39 blue marbles and 52 red ones. Who can make a pattern in the ratio of 3 : 4 (blue : red) and use all of their marbles?

_____

1 mark

PS **3** The sides of this rectangle are in the ratio 1 : 3. The sides are scaled up by a factor of 5. What are the lengths of the sides of the new rectangle?

3 cm

_____

2 marks

Marks.......... /8

Total marks .... /26   How am I doing? 😊 😐 😖

73

Solving Equations

1 $x + 5 = 12$ $x =$ _____   1 mark

2 What are the next three numbers in the sequence?

  3   6   9   _____   _____   _____   1 mark

3 $y - 3 = 24$ $y =$ _____   1 mark

4 $2x = 16$ $x =$ _____   1 mark

5 If $x = 3$, find the value of $5x + 10$ _____   1 mark

6 $2x + 5 = 11$ $x =$ _____   1 mark

7 $a + b = 5$. List all the numbers that a and b could be.   2 marks

_____

8 Complete the table. One has been done for you.

n	$3n + 2$
1	5
5	
10	
20	
100	

4 marks

Marks.........../12

1 $3x + 5 = 20$ $x =$ _____   1 mark

2 What is the rule for this sequence?

    12   17   22   27

_____   1 mark

3 $20 - 2y = 14$ $y =$ _____   1 mark

4 $ab = 12$. List all the possible numbers that a and b could be.   2 marks

_____

Solving Equations

5 If $x = 7$, work out $5x - 14$. _____

1 mark

6 What are the next three terms in this sequence?

13   7   1   _____   _____   _____

3 marks

7 $a + b = 15$ and $a - b = 7$

$a =$ _____ $b =$ _____

2 marks

Marks.......... /11

Challenge 3

1 What is the rule for this sequence?

_____

1 mark

2 $3a + 23 = 107$ $a =$ _____

1 mark

3 $ab - 3 = 21$. List all the possible numbers for a and b.

_____

4 marks

4 What is the next term in this sequence?

3   9   21   45   _____

1 mark

5 Complete the table.

n	$2n + 5$	$3n$	$100n$
5			
		45	
	25		
			60

4 marks

Marks.......... /11

Total marks .... /34   How am I doing?

1 a) Plot these points: A(2,5) B(4,5) C(2,1)

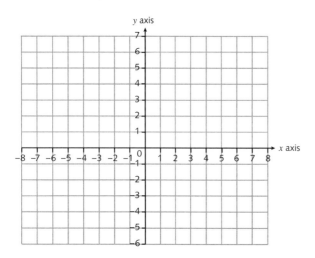

y axis

x axis

3 marks

b) ABCD is a rectangle. Plot point D.

1 mark

c) What are the coordinates of point D?

_____

1 mark

d) Translate ABCD to A'B'C'D' by moving it 6 squares left and 5 squares down.

1 mark

e) Write down the coordinates of:

A'(___ , ___)   B'(___ , ___)   C'(___ , ___)   D'(___ , ___)

4 marks

2 Convert these fractions to percentages.

a) $\frac{12}{20}$ _____   **b)** $\frac{7}{25}$ _____   **c)** $\frac{8}{40}$ _____

3 marks

3 The mean of three numbers is 7. What is the third number?

6   5   _____

1 mark

4 Mina plays in three matches. In the first she scores three goals, in the second she scores one goal and in the last game she scores five goals. What is the average number of goals she scored?

_____

1 mark

PS 5 Paul's recipe for meatballs is for 10 people. How much does he need of each ingredient if he only wants to make enough for four people?

For 10 people		For 4 people	
Beef	120 g	Beef	_____
Tomato sauce	100 g	Tomato sauce	_____
Onions	50 g	Onions	_____

3 marks

6 Reflect shape A in the y axis to become A'. Give the coordinates for the vertices of shape A'.

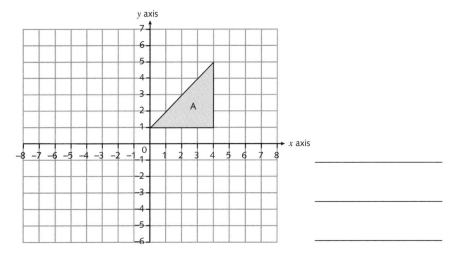

_____

_____

_____

3 marks

7 $4^3 - 7^2$ = _____

1 mark

8 Circle the ratio equivalent to $4:15$.

8:23   12:45   8:35   12:30

1 mark

9 $ab = 14$

a and b are prime numbers. a and b = ?

a = _____ b = _____

2 marks

10 $3a + 13 = 37$ a = _____

1 mark

11 Complete the table.

n	5*n*	4*n* – 3
6		
		37
	45	

3 marks

12 Year 7 measured how much it rained for one week.

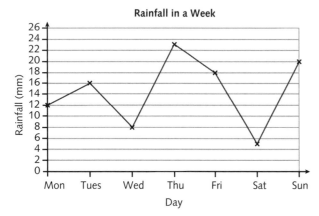

Rainfall in a Week

a) What units are the rainfall measured in? _____

b) How many measurements did Year 7 take? _____

c) On how many days did it rain more than 10 mm? _____

d) What was the total rainfall for the whole week? _____

e) What is the mean rainfall for Monday, Tuesday and Wednesday?

_____

1 mark

1 mark

1 mark

1 mark

1 mark

13 $\frac{1}{4} \times \frac{1}{5} =$ ☐

1 mark

PS **14** Here is part of a bus timetable:

	Bus A	Bus B	Bus C	Bus D
Poyser Avenue	8:15	9:50	11:15	12:30
St. Katherine's Close	9:45	–	12:30	14:15
Gregory Boulevard	11:35	12:55	13:55	–
King William Yard	13:50	14:10	15:05	17:15

a) Which bus takes the longest time to travel from Poyser Avenue to King William Yard?

_____

b) Which is the quickest bus? _____

c) Kate catches a bus that leaves Poyser Avenue before 12 noon and arrives at King William Yard after 3 p.m.

Which bus did she catch? _____

d) Jackie is meeting a friend in Gregory Boulevard for coffee at 3 p.m.

Which is the latest bus she could catch? _____

PS **15** Shape ABCD is a square. Give the coordinates of B, C and D.

B (_____ , _____)

C (_____ , _____)

D (_____ , _____)

16 Fill in the boxes on the number line.

0.98   1.1

17 The temperature inside a freezer is −18°C. The freezer is in a kitchen which is at a temperature of 19°C.

What is the temperature difference between the freezer and the kitchen?

_____ °C

18 There are 76 469 fans at a football match. Round this to the nearest thousand.

_____

Progress Test 4

PS Problem-solving questions

19 Estimate the size of this angle. Tick the correct answer.

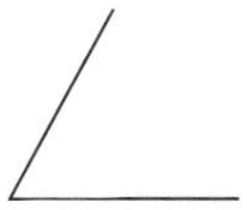

30° ☐ 90° ☐ 60° ☐ 100° ☐

1 mark

PS **20** Calculate the area of this shape.

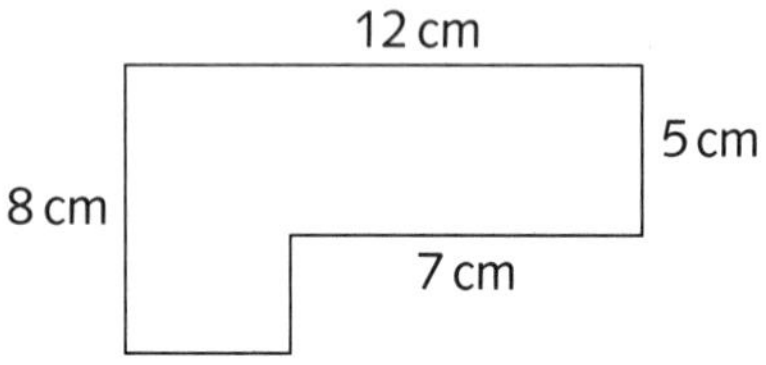

12 cm
5 cm
8 cm
7 cm

A = ________ cm^2

1 mark

PS **21** What is the volume of this cube?

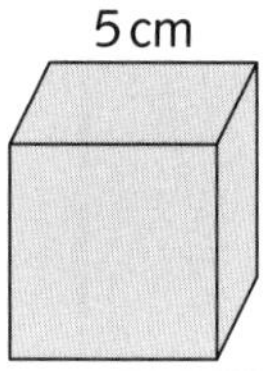

5 cm

V = ________ cm^3

1 mark

22 What 3-D shape will this net make?

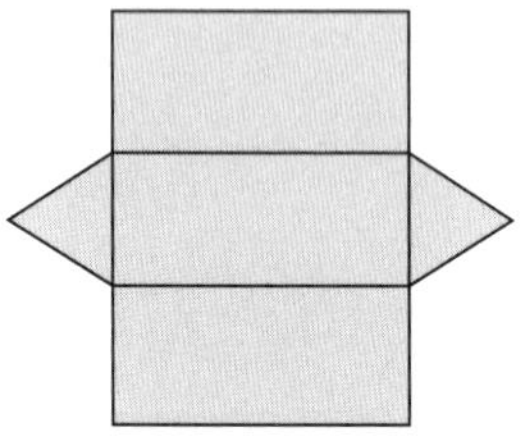

____

1 mark

PS **23** Mina takes her chocolate cake out of the oven at 7.45 p.m. It baked for 2 hours and 25 minutes.

What time did she put it in the oven?

____

1 mark

Marks......... /51